BREAKING SHACKLES

THE STORY OF THE LOWLY DISHWASHER

JERRY READY

PAGE PUBLISHING, INC.
Conneaut Lake, PA

First originally published by Page Publishing 2021

ISBN 978-1-64544-532-6 (pbk)
ISBN 978-1-64544-533-3 (digital)

Printed in the United States of America

MISSION STATEMENT

While some may need more work than others it is a hard fight to taste the fruit of our fathers tree. Yet as it is possible I want to be clear and make no mistake about it that which was lost has been found. Through rigorous practice seeking a higher consciousness there and only there one can find noble truths and spiritual wisdom and so. The Jerry Ready foundation offers liberation through meditation and yoga ect. Teaching divine mental and physical awareness, while at the same time cultivating the necessary skills needed to reach oneness with self.

CHAPTER ONE

Rehab

As I lay in my bunk bed a few days freshly removed from a level one to a level four prison facility. I happen to find myself overly compelled by something greater than myself to write my life experiences in a book. I say "overly compelled" because writing a book and seeing it through was just not for seeable and or possible being honest. Considering that I had a third-grade reading level at the age of twenty-eight, I was in my eighth year of incarceration. As crazy as that thought was, jumping off the top bunk, reaching into my locker, I grabbed my special folder that I would write my daily journals in. Sitting at a desk as my cellmate watched his TV with his headphones on, as those were the rules, I started writing from my earliest memory.

Life for me was typical growing up as a child, my earliest memories were my six brothers and sisters getting up, dressing for school if it was a weekend night. We would raid the parties my parents had the night before.

I, being different, found myself the only one eating the ashes out the ashtray or eating the end of used matches. Everything they did during those loud parties was exposed to us early, and at free will, we had our own parties after they went to bed.

Life seemed easy but fast, being the middle child growing up. I felt the need for a lot of attention but found none at home, having six other siblings;

Once my brothers and I got in our teenage years, we started living the fast life; there was no turning back. Girls, gangs, drugs, and alcohol—we believed we were untouchable.

It did not take long for the life of drugs and alcohol that we were exposed to start to affect our lives. By the age of thirteen, my oldest brother was on his way to prison for multiple gun charges. I found myself following in his footsteps.

I was drinking alcohol and smoking before the age of twelve. I remember my aunt being there as I woke up with my first hangover. Mom found me the night before and thought I was dead. She found me naked in a pool of my own vomit; she called the police where I drunkenly told them who got me drunk.

I'd always felt when the time came that I needed to stop, I could go cold turkey. In this case, my child Cam Cam was born. I had told Crissy the mother of our child that when he was born, I would stop using drugs.

Things only got worse for me, added to the fact. I also was being unfaithful, staying out nights at a time, not being there for my family.

It wasn't too long after that I started hitting Crissy, we would start arguing, which made me choose to hit her even more at times.

Finally, Crissy did get tired of the way I was treating her. She gave me an ultimatum, asking of me to stop living the fast life, stop doing drugs, and seek help or I had to leave.

I loved Crissy, so I chose help, through friends and family. I was enrolled to the Salvation Army Rehab Center, a residential placement where I had to stay fifteen days without leaving.

Between the ages of ten and twenty-one, I had already done just about every drug, including prescription medications (uppers and downers) except for meth and heroin, mixing them with alcohol and marijuana.

Having one day, before I had to report to the rehab center, at the last minute I decided that I did not want to go. As much as we fought, I did not want to be apart from Crissy, even though we both were cheating on each other at that time, I did not want to be without her for that long,

I also did not want to change; as bad as my life was at that point—I had lost everything—I still was not ready to stop living the lifestyle that I became accustomed to living.

The friends helping me through the process of going to rehab were Thomas and Cynthia. They were older than I was, but most of my friends for as long as I can remember have always been older than me.

Cynthia was the mother to Thomas's eldest child Thomas Junior. I lived in their basement. That evening, neither Thomas nor Cynthia knew I called Crissy to come visit me the day before I had to report to the rehab center, which was not a problem, what they did not know was that I planned on leaving with her when she came.

She came to the house, I told her how I was planning on going back with her. We started arguing out loud; it was not long before Thomas and Cynthia was in the argument as well. Cynthia took Crissy upstairs while I stayed in the basement, crying to Thomas about how I did not want to go to rehab.

Upon going upstairs, Cynthia had already put Crissy into the car to send her home, finding that out, I was hurt and let down. Words can't describe the emotions that felt in that moment, I cried like a baby.

After a while, Thomas had to go to work, so I just talked with Cynthia. We started drinking Jim Beam right out the bottle. We sat there by the fireplace till she came up with the whole idea of going down to the local bar.

I was not old enough to get in or drink; Cynthia told me not to worry about that. I felt since I was going to rehab, why not? I had no money to spend, so she gave me twenty dollars to spend how I wanted to. I could play pool very well, and this was my first time in a bar.

Needless to say, I started doing well, and people started buying me drinks, every time my glass was low, sometimes even random people that I was not even playing pool with was sending drinks over; in truth, I found that so cool.

The turning point that evening was trying to smoke. I had smoked marijuana on a constant basis since age of twelve. I was very familiar with the smell, and smoking it, I knew something was wrong. Something had been slipped on me. I felt a way that I had never felt before. I had to leave, step out to get some fresh air to recompose myself.

I must have stood out there for two hours or so until Cynthia came out. I don't remember when or how we got home that night.

The next day was the start of rehab. After washing my clothes, getting cigarettes and my calling cards, it was time to go. After getting dropped off, giving hugs and kisses, I was greeted by a lady that told me the rules and showed me around the rehab center. My room, lunch room, workout room, and the place where we would be having our daily group meetings.

After all the small pleasantries were done, I had to turn in all my personal belongings. I learned that the lady that was doing my intake was the aunt of one of my old roommates that did make me feel better being in this unknown place.

After getting settled in, I decided to reach out to Crissy to let her know that I was in the rehab center and safe. I was not able to reach her; I was very upset about that. In truth, I feared she was with another man, which added to the fact none of our mutual friends were able to get hold of her.

I was starting to get depressed. I did nothing but stay in my room, feeling sick from not being with her, not knowing what she was doing or who she was with. After a while, I finally decided to come out the room for dinner. I started seeing the people that I would be living with for the next fifteen days. The first thing that I noticed was the heroin addicts and the things I had seen them going through with their withdrawals. It was one of the craziest things I had seen up close in person. I swore then that I would never do heroin.

In that moment, I put myself above the people there. I had this notion that I was not as bad as they were, and I really believed that.

So I started to think of a way to leave. It was time to go. I really did not give the rehab center a chance.

It was that night in my room I had a strong feeling in a funny way, something big was going to happen; something was going to change in my life. While trying to formulate a plan on how to leave, I decided not to go to my group meetings. Besides the fact I did not want to talk with anyone till I found a way to leave, I just wanted to be left alone. All I wanted to do was sleep or just lie there and look at the wall, counting bricks. My roommate was constantly trying to get me to go to group. At first I did blow him off, not caring. After hearing him talk for two days, I finally agreed to go.

Group was held two times a day. For a while, I just sat there within my own thoughts or I would just listen. The people talked about things that I thought was mind blowing. While working out in the gym talking with another person, I found out that everyone else had been court-ordered to be at the rehab center. I was one of the few, if not the only one there, that could just walk out anytime I wanted. If I was trying to leave, I thought that was good to know.

The next group, one of the other members' family, came to sit in on one of the meetings. It was allowed for family members to come and sit in on our meetings. One of the family members' daughters looked my age if not older; she just stared at me. Every time I looked over, she was looking at me. I thought to myself, *She is very attractive.* I found myself feeling very embarrassed. And out of place, I got up and went to my room to start looking for someone to come get me. I was not staying in this place any longer.

CHAPTER TWO

The Fall

My list of people to help me was pretty much slim to none. Crissy was not going to come get me, neither would Thomas or Cynthia or James, an old roommate that worked at the post office with his mother. I gave him a call and found out that tomorrow he was not working but his mother would. I asked to talk to her, and she said that after work, she would be there to pick me up. I did not know if she knew that she was picking me up from the rehab center. I did not care; I was ready to go home.

The next morning, I went to the intake lady to let her know that afternoon I would be departing the rehab center. She advised me to stay and give the place a real chance. Truth was, I had my mind made up already. It was time to go. I missed Crissy and was already homesick.

Later that day, my ride did come. I was so happy to be out of that place. We stopped at Burger King and hit the highway. We arrived at Crissy's apartment around dinnertime. She was not happy to see me. I could see that reading her body language. She also knew that I was supposed to be there for fifteen days. That might have had something to do with her anger as well. Surprisingly, we did not fight. I was too tired, and I think she was as well.

After dinner, I asked Crissy if I could take her car and go to a friend's house. My truck and car were both in the impound reluctantly. She gave me the keys to go. I went to a young lady that was my mistress at the time. Crissy and Jade knew about each other. I had been caught red-handed a few times.

My money was funny. At the time, I had no place to take her. We ended up going to my mother's house in the city, parked, and made out. We talked a little, then I took her home shortly after. The next day, Crissy left me home to watch Cameron while she went to work. I sat there and played the game, drinking beer, enjoying the day with my son. Crissy arrived home at around four o'clock in the afternoon. I asked to take the car and go somewhere. We instantly started arguing. The next thing I knew, I had lost control of myself. I started pulling her hair. Punching her in the face hard but not hard enough to leave bruises, I dragged her from the living room to the back bedroom where I slammed her on the bed and choked her till she gasped, begging me to stop. With my arms still around her, I told her to take off her clothes.

After we settled down, I found myself crying, telling her I apologized for all the things I had put her through. I felt less of a man. While holding me in her arms, she told me she forgave me. I don't know if she was telling the truth or not; nonetheless, I felt really bad and had to leave. Crissy insisted that I should not leave, that we should work things out; I asked for the keys and left.

I stopped at our local gas station to use the phone to call my mistress Jade to see if she wanted to get together. I was short on gas. She did not have any money, so we decided to get together another day.

I did happen to see another old friend while at the gas station, Jenna. We had been friends since twelve. She was due to have her first baby soon. I stayed and talked to her for a few. After a while, she could tell something was troubling me. She asked me to come over after she got out of work. Still upset, I ended up going to the country, where I grew up.

I happened to run into a family member. Buck and I used to be inseparable growing up till we all got girlfriends. We started talking about smoking weed, clearing our minds, but we both had no money. Buck said something about robbing the weed man. I was even convinced that the police would not get called. I definitely was not in my right mind, out of character surprisingly. I said, "Forget it—let's do it."

We did not want to go to the door, we also needed a getaway driver. At that moment, Fats walked in another childhood friend. After telling him about our plan for the robbery, we asked if he wanted in; he said yes.

We got in my car to scope the place out. I went to the door to see if she was selling anything, while Buck and Fats stayed in the car. Only the lady was there, we headed back to the country to find someone brave enough to kick the door down. Just then, we ran into Poo. Poo was older than us and a crack addict, someone we could trust. If offered the right price, he would agree to it.

Buck went and acquired the ammunition, a .38 revolver for me and a military .45 assault rifle for Poo. Fats went and got the change of clothes, two hats with the eyes ripped out, and new shirts. Surprisingly, in the car on the way there, Buck tried to give me every reason as to why we should not be doing this. At that point, I did not care and had made my mind up, so I told him it was still going to happen.

When we got there, Buck and Fats parked up the street a block away, while Poo and I walked to the house. When we got to the porch, we turned our backs and stood at the door, where I proceeded to knock. She came to the door and must have thought we was on something out of the ordinary. The first thing that she spoke was, "If you two do not turn around and tell me who you are, I'm going to call the police." With one eye cut out of our hats, backs to the door, I knocked again. That's when she got on the phone to call the police.

At this point, I have to say reality was starting to kick in. As scared as I was, I stood my ground. Poo then turned around and took off his hat so the lady could see his face. I watched, stunned and transfixed, while he kicked the door down. After three kicks, Poo was gun in hand, chasing the lady around the house. I stood frozen, never pulling my gun from my pocket.

Poo told her to give him the stuff we had come for, while she ran around the house, screaming with her hands in the air. I can remember the newborn baby crying from the back room. She then fell to the floor next to the entertainment system in the living room. Reaching in one of the cabinets, she pulled out what was at that time the biggest bag of marijuana I had ever seen at one time.

Before I saw it touch Poo's hand, I was running out the door to the alley where the car was parked. Soon as I was in the car, Poo was right behind me and started equally handing out the marijuana. I told him to stop; we had done all the dirty work. We had to get more.

We started back to the country where we first got together. We decided to go to my grandparents' house. We jumped out of the car to go our own ways. Fats jumped across the hood of a car in the street to reach Perry's car, Buck went to his sister's house across the street, and Poo seemed to have just disappeared. I ran to the window of my grandparents' house and passed the guns and clothes through window to my brother John.

I turned, watching Perry and Fats pulling off. Perry was a friend of both sides of the family, mine and the victims of the robbery, as I was. Till that moment, I never really took into account what that meant—her being mutual friends or how she would react. I knew Fats would tell her everything down to detail what we had done—that was Fats.

Everyone was sleeping at my grandparents' house. I proceeded to my Aunt Catherine's house where I smoked some of the marijuana we got. Talking to Cookie my godfather and Aunt Catherine, they told me I was wrong for any role I played to get what I had.

Buck knocked at the door to tell me he started to see police driving around the projects (the country) since they did not have a presence like that. I knew something was odd; they may be looking for us.

I felt it was time to split from the county with Buck. I called James to pick up Crissy to bring her to me. By the time they had gotten there, Crissy knew everything. She was very mad, but then what could she do? What was done was done.

She arrived to see the police steady. Driving around, I thought it best to get Crissy back home. maybe not the best ideal on my behalf, but I had her leave Cam Cam with me.

Shortly after, I received a call from James, telling me that Crissy house was being raided, she had gotten arrested with the car going to the impound for investigation. That's when I knew I was in trouble.

James took me and Cam Cam to Mary's, my brother Luckie's girlfriend's, house to lie low for a while to try to figure things out. When I got to my brother's, I told him everything that I did. Upset as he was, he told me I had a place to stay for as long as I needed. We smoked and talked. After a while, it was getting late and Cameron was getting harder and harder to control, so I called my brother Brock and Ella to take Cameron for the night.

My brother did not have a phone, so every time that I needed to use the phones, I had to go down the street to use Amber's phone. I had nowhere to turn and no one to talk to, so I called Bella, Crissy's stepmother. I told her everything and left nothing out; she told me everything was going to be okay.

Going back to my brother's house, I smoked a joint and went to sleep. I woke up a few hours later with the house surrounded by cops with guns; my brother came down the stairs in just enough time to tell me the police was there, to hide any drugs I had. I looked to see if there was a way to run, but there was not. I acted as if I was asleep in the chair in the corner of the basement; three minutes later as I heard them running down the stairs, I was instantly surrounded by a face full of guns that moment reminded me of a movie I had seen growing up.

After being handcuffed, they read me my rights to take me in. In the process, the police had raided four houses looking for me: my grandparents' house, Crissy's house, the house of my brother's girlfriend, and where I was using the phone down the street from my brothers.

I ran into Poo in the county building. While I was being processed, he had been caught the night of the robbery. I had no idea how I had gotten caught; I thought Poo or someone else had told. He was wearing the same clothes from the robbery. The lady we robbed had picked him out in a police lineup, he told me. He was trying to see if I told anything. I made a statement telling the whole story under the belief the police was there to help me. At the age of twenty, I had no idea about the justice system. The police had all they needed to hold us both. I was sick.

CHAPTER THREE

The New Way

I woke the next morning to Crissy making bail. I tried everything to get her attention; she did not see me in the cell right behind her I. was hurt watching her leave. At the time, I had not been charged with anything yet. It was more of a waiting game.

I remember when I was a kid going to school, we took field trips to the county building. I told myself I would never be locked down while walking the halls, my first time seeing inside being locked up in rawness. Little did I know that would be the first of a lot of things I would do I thought I would never do.

Being in the holding cell was hell for me. I spent the next three days in there. One guy passed away right in front of the cell. From what was told to us later, he drank too much. There were fights for almost everything. In truth, it was frightening, cold, and very uncomfortable. All I was wearing was what they arrested me in, a V-neck T-shirt and pajama pants, which added to the fact we all slept between the floor, brick, or steel seats.

At the arraignment, Monday morning, I was being charged with carrying a concealed weapon, Felony firearm, assault with intent to rob while armed, and first-degree home invasion. I had never done time in jail. As an adolescent, when I was fifteen or sixteen, I did do a day or so in the youth home, but jail was a whole different story.

My stepfather was there, along with an old friend of the family, Sonny. Since I could not afford an attorney, nor could anyone. In my family, the courts provided me with a court-appointed one. The court proceeding was not for me to plead my case; it was to see if the circuit court had enough evidence to send me to a higher court for some of the felonies I might be charged with.

They had all the evidence they needed. I was sent to the higher courts with the bond of half a million cash or five thousand cash with an assistance of a house or a very nice car, something along those lines. I was told it was so high because if I ran the bail, bondsman would be able to keep the money. It really did not matter. I had burned all my bridges with everyone. No one was going to put that up for me; I was there to stay.

Monday night, I was taken upstairs to a twelve-man cell. I was thinking about how to explain that I was not in the right state of mind when we committed the robbery. How could I say it to get out of trouble? It was a big question for me because I understood what I did was wrong; I had been seeing mental health services for as long as I could remember. Being naïve, I convinced myself it made sense to play that role, going into this process with jail and my case.

I missed home; it was very hard to sleep at night. I had been so used to sleeping next to someone I found nights most depressing. When I found myself at that point, thoughts of hurting myself became all too real. Suddenly, I did not care how much trouble I was really into because I played the class clown in jail. Before the week was out, I had talked to my mother, Jade, and my aunt Linda, who was very close to me. Crissy's stepmom and dad took my calls as well. Crissy's phone was not set up to take collect calls at that time, so I would call Jade and have her call three-way for me to talk to Crissy.

In truth, I was trying to get anyone that was mutual friends with the people we robbed to not testify against me at the same time. No one was trying to make bail. Neither she nor my family members stepped up to help. I really was surprised when no one would help me get a paid lawyer.

Jade was being more of my woman than Crissy was. I don't think Crissy wrote me a letter the first two months I was in there. I started praying a lot, thinking God would somehow get me out of the trouble I was in.

By now, I had gotten to know my cellmates, mostly the ones that were in trouble like I was, small-timers who left as fast as they came. I had been in the county jail for a few weeks before I got any money. Jade had sent me a few dollars. Crissy's mom, Bella, told me she would send me a money order. Before the money even came, I ate it up with the sucker store. You go to an inmate; he gives you a bag of chips that cost $1.00. Now you would have to pay him back $1.50 to $2.00 interest, depending on what he wanted. I had run a bill for the whole money order that was being sent to me.

Then I thought, *Forget that*. I was not going to pay what I owed. I started to put a plan in motion to get moved to a different cell so that I wouldn't have to pay the guys money. I had seen tons of fights by now. The sucker store inmate had beaten up an inmate that tried to bully me. I was wrong for what I was about to do next. I had been seeing mental health for as long as I could remember; there was a mental health six-man cell across the hall. My brother was over there, He wasn't my brother by birth. When we were kids, my mom took him in and let him live with us. Since then, we have called each other brothers.

I was trying to get moved to that cell. When the police guards came to do their rounds. While everybody else was doing other things, I asked if he could call me out and speak to me, he said yes. When he came to the door and called me out the holding cell, it got quiet. The only person that knew what I was going to do was my bunkie. When I got into the office, I told the officer about how I was seeing mental health, how I was starting to get depressed about my case, I went on telling him all kinds of BS until he stopped me and said he had a place to move me. I had already known where I was going right across the hall. When me and the officer got back to the cell, he told me while the door was closed that he was going to do the paperwork to move me and it would be ten to fifteen minutes. The officer opened the door and closed it. The inmate that I was trying to rip off was like, "Hell no, I know you are not moving." I guess he assumed it right off.

I had to improvise. I said no, no, it was a phone call about my mother. I made up some lie right off the top of my head, but just like clockwork, the officer came right back, opened the door, and said, "Mr. Ready, pack your things. You're moving."

I asked the officer if he would stay there while I got my things together because I didn't want anything to happen to me. That other inmate had to be very upset because the next day, the store was coming and he was going to get my whole bag. Since the police was right there, there wasn't too much he could say out loud about his private store because he would get into trouble, so he asked for my tokens. I told him not to worry. Tomorrow, I had every intention of paying him, which I really did not. He said, "Okay, just make sure you keep your word." So there I was in the six man cell with my brother; I didn't know anyone else in that cell. I didn't need to; my brother was there. All that night, we talked and caught up on all the old times. I told him about my case. He told me about his. He was in there for CSC. I can't remember if it was first or second degree, but whether or not, it was not good because the crime had been done to his child. I knew that it was a hard subject to talk about, so I never asked him about it again.

The next day, we got store. The guards passed food and hygiene products through the bars very early in the morning. When it was my turn to receive my store bag, the guard asked me if I had anything for someone across the hall. I said, "Hell no" for the officer to ask and willing to pass store goods. He knew it was a debt I needed to pay. In response to his expression, I looked shocked and said okay. After the officer left, we were served chow (lunch); the slots in the doors was appropriated. From my bed, I could hear the inmate calling me, but I acted like I was sleeping. Clearly, he was upset. He started calling names, telling me about what he would do at first. I just kept playing like I was asleep, and then he talked about my mother. That's when I went to the slot. I told him to get paid or get it how he lived, which in prison terms means I would not pay and for him to act next. We shared words for a while until they closed the slots, but I knew if the dude got his hands on me, he would hurt me bad.

Jade stopped writing me, sending me money, and taking my phone calls. By now, she was all I had. My other family members weren't taking my calls either. Sometimes I would get lucky and call over Bella and Joe's house and catch Crissy and Cameron, which was nice because we were still together. With no one to talk to, I found myself into the Bible deep. I knew I was in trouble; I felt that with prayer, God would see me through this.

I believed we were trying to get a lawyer; at first, I was told her name was Shon Cook. A female, she wanted way too much money for me and Crissy to afford. I hoped that Bella and Joe would come around and help me get a lawyer. They wanted me out of Crissy's life and made it very clear getting me a lawyer was out the question.

Reading my transcripts, it was hard truly understanding, as mad as Bella was, that she wanted me out of Crissy's life; she wrote a statement against me. Crissy did as well. They were prosecutors number one and two to testify against me if I took it to trial.

A court-appointed lawyer came to see me a while later. Not Shon Cook, one of the lawyers from her office. We spoke about the case, what I did, what I did not do, and how much time I was looking at. He told me that since this was my first felony; at worst, he could get me six years. Never having done time, I was shocked and refused. That moment, I still did not understand how deep in trouble I was. I knew that what I did was wrong, but no one had gotten hurt. Nothing got taken. Well, that's what they thought anyways. What was I about to do so much time for?

He told me that boot camp was still on the table, teen challenge as well. A religious placement was strict, but if I could get them to accept me, it would look fantastic. So he was speaking good and bad. I had to wait and see. In the process, he told me he would try to get me a deal to plead guilty for a lesser time. I told him goodbye. I never saw him again.

The court had other plans for me. They took it upon themselves to fire him and gave me another lawyer. At this point, it was all a waiting game. As I got comfortable being there, I played around for the next few months. We used to do anything for a laugh. Sometimes I would get everybody up to play spades. I would be naked. Everyone else would sit there like everything was okay, like this was something we did every day. We would wait until we heard officers' keys on the rock (walking, making their rounds) then we would play cards and wait to see their reactions; most were funny as hell.

It was customary to put up a sheet using the bathrooms; we would put sheets up to cover us like a wall. I would just sit there, putting nothing up. We would laugh so hard; they loved me for that. I used to put turbans on my head and wrap sheets around me like I was a Muslim. They thought I was crazy. There was a porter (an inmate that cleans around jail) I did not get along with. We had words; we beefed every day after that until I left.

One day, when I was praying with some guys, he sprayed me with some cleaner in a bottle; that really had me upset. The next morning, when it was his time to clean, I lined up ten balls, toilet paper dipped in yellow toilet water. I waited as soon as he came around. I hit him in the face and body with them, I sent him running. That was very funny. The next time he got me good. I was not paying attention when he slapped me across the face with a broom. That was nasty as hell and pissed me off once again. I waited for about a week or two before I got him back. I asked a few of my jail mates to help me; they had pictures of naked women. I had like four of them standing next to the bars. While he was looking at the girls, I reached between them, and as hard as I could, I slapped the hell out of that porter. Everybody laughed; that was funny. I did that to him. Another time, he got mad enough and asked for peace, so we made peace.

Crissy came to see me around this time. Visits were only an hour, and only two people could come at a time. Sometimes she would bring her friends Kim and Amy. One other time, she brought Howard; he was a friend I went to school with. By this time, I did not know how much, but I understood I would do some kind of prison term. Every time she came to see me, I used to just tell her if she would leave me then make it easy for us both and do it now. She said it did not matter how much time I had she was there to stay, and I believed her.

By now, I had met my new lawyer. He told me nothing new; he expressed to me he was trying to get me a deal. I still was praying and reading the Bible. God would get me out of the mess I was in, or that was what I believed anyway. Remember the inmate I ripped off for that money? Well, turns out he had friends in high places because I was locked down in a holding cell with him downstairs. Don't know why I was in that cell in the first place. All I remember was seeing his face and him hitting me in my face after that. I remember waking up back in my cell upstairs. Crazy, right? I guess I had that coming; that's when my brother and me started working out.

Being in a cell, there were only a few things we could do: push-ups, pull-ups, and sit-ups. The goal was to get stronger so that never happened again.

There was a girl cell next door to ours; they would send us letters, and we would send them letters. We were buying pills to get high; they would send their underwear to us. Mostly, they were just fun to talk to.

The whole cell had flipped. My brother and I were the only ones left from when I had first moved into the cell. Paul, a friend I grew up with, had gotten locked up for strong armed robbery. I knew him from the streets, so I talked to him a lot.

While going through my pictures, he said he recognized Crissy. He told me all kinds of things that him and his friends used to do with her and her friends; I was sick. I felt like I wanted to vomit.

This hurt my feelings. When I saw Crissy on our next visit, she said none of it was true. I knew she was lying. Paul knew too much—her friends' names, where our apartment was, my son's name, everything.

This is when I took sleeping pills. I'd snort them then crush them in coffee just to get high. I didn't care at this point; this was around the time I tried to commit suicide. In school, I learned that enough pencil lead can kill a person, and that's what I tried to kill myself with. I broke down like ten pencils, put the lead in water, and cried to my brother and just drank. I truly believed I would die. I was just laughed at. Everybody knew the pencil lead would not kill me; they wanted to see how far I went—that was that.

The next day, I called my mom and told her how I was feeling and what I had done. She knew I had been into the Bible and praying a lot; she sent a member of the church to see me. My mother is a reformed Mormon. I had no problem with that; it's what made her happy. I did not like how she used to wake me and my brothers and sisters up at five o'clock in the morning to read from the Bible and book of Mormon. The member from the church came to see me; we talked and prayed. Before he departed, he left me a book of Mormon.

My court date was in the next few days. Around that time, I was working out, reading the Bible, and preparing myself for the outcome. I can recall going downstairs to see my lawyer the day before my court date; this would be a day I'd always remember. While I was in the holding cell, Whitehall High School brought a field trip in just like they did when I was a kid. I recall seeing a little boy I used to babysit. His name was Lloyd. I waved at him; seeing him was unexpected.

I was summoned to see my lawyer, as the guard walked me from my cell down the stairs, I really did not know what to expect. He was a court-appointed lawyer. From that alone, I really did not expect much out of him. I was very hopeful; he had good news motivated only by faith and prayer. As I sat into the chair the guard put me in, the man with the suitcase turned around, saying he was my lawyer. He told me without stopping, and I quote, he proclaimed he could not beat my case if I took it to trial. He stated I would be found guilty and get life. He went on to say his plea agreement had been made already, and it was the only one to be offered. If I pleaded guilty, I would receive eleven to thirty years in prison—five to twenty years for the home invasion, nine to thirty years for the assault with the intention to rob while armed, and two years for the gun charge. I told him, hell no, that was not possible and that was too much time. He said it was all he could offer me. I needed to put serious thought in this decision. I did not have to have an answer until my court date tomorrow. I asked him if I could use his cell phone to call Crissy. At first, he said no. I told him about how I needed to talk to her, and he kindly let me use the phone.

When I called, Crissy was not home. I returned back upstairs to think about everything my lawyer had just told me. I kept everything that discussed between us to myself; he said he would try to get a better deal. In truth, I was hoping for the best but expecting the worst. The next morning, I called my mom. I told her how I was feeling and what I had done.

I kept everything that was said between us to myself. When I woke up, everybody else was already up in the cell. There were a few of us going downstairs to get sentenced, so we prayed. Not long after, I was taken to the courtroom. Crissy, Cameron, Kim (Crissy's friend), my sister Dashia, my mom, and her husband were all there.

The first thing they did was took me into the back room to talk with my lawyer. He told me the same thing he told me the night before: he could not beat the charges. If I did not take what was offered to me, I would get life in prison.

He proceeded by telling me he could get one of the gun charges dropped; the time offered would remain the same. He explained I had made the statement against myself and there was really nothing I could do. I had to take the time offered, or that's what I was told. Things could have been different for me if I had a paid lawyer, but I didn't. I told my lawyer to tell Crissy and my mom what was going on. Up until that point, everything had been okay for me. Hearing and understanding that I was about to do or serve the next eleven years of my life behind bars had not really hit me yet. That was until I saw the reaction of Crissy, and my mother crying. Crissy stormed out of the courtroom; I knew then it was not a dream. I put my head down and started crying. I sat there in the jury stand until it was my turn to go in front of the judge.

While accepting my plea, the judge asked me if there was anything I wanted to say. I said sorry to the family I robbed, sorry to my family for the embarrassment that I had put them through. After all was done, I was sentenced to my time: one hundred and thirty-eight months with the max time of thirty years. Five to twenty years for the home invasion first degree, nine years to thirty for assault with intent to rob while armed, along with two years for the felony firearm.

Ashamed of my shackles, I was ushered out of the courtroom and said my goodbyes to everyone there in the courtroom. Arriving at my cell, so many different emotions were built up. I went straight to the bed facing the wall and cried again. No one said anything to me because they pretty much already knew what I was going through. They understood I just needed some time alone. As I lay there, I started thinking about how much time I had to do in prison. At that time, I could not see the end. Eleven years? That sounded so long. That time I was fifteen or sixteen years old and passing through the youth home—one day here, one day there, seeing those guys having to stay without leaving for years. They were the first people I thought about.

I also thought about the things that I would miss the most. Crissy was at the top, even though all we did was fight. I guess you could say in my own way I loved her. Not being able to be with her any more was something I was not ready to accept or even try to think about. I also thought about the effect all this would have on Cameron. I hurt so much for my boy. He did not ask to be brought into this world Now, because of my dumb and selfish actions, for some of the best years of his life, he would be fatherless. Needless to say, I had a lot on my mind. All that day, I did not eat or sleep; I just sat there looking at the wall.

After a while, I got up told my brother and few other guys what had transpired. No one was surprised; everyone knew I had some time coming. My brother's court date was next. I took the few pictures that were sent to me. I put them in a book; the day before I was to ride out to prison. Once sentenced, the following Friday, you're sent to quarantine. So I tried to enjoy the time we had left with each other.

I was to ride out the next morning. The visit was good, as well as the timing; they had just got done fixing up the county building. Babies could be brought into visits; it was the first time I seen Cameron since I caught the case. Walking in, he stood on the visiting table behind a window. He was handsome and seemed to not recognize me. I spent most of that visit watching my son. He had gotten big. In the few months I was gone, it felt like he did not know who I was—that hurt. Nonetheless, I was happy to see my boy; that was all that mattered. As the visit came to an end, Crissy told me she loved me and would be there for me to see this through. She told me to look out the window when I made it back to my cell; she had a surprise for me. From the window, I could see Burger King's parking lot when she pulled up; my brother and Buck were in the car. They got out and waved toward the county building. In that moment, I was happy to see them. At the same time, it truly felt bittersweet.

CHAPTER FOUR

Quarantine

Everything that was in my possession had to be sent home or given away. I was told to make arrangements as I would be transferred to the custody of the MDOC, the Michigan Department of Corrections. My food and hygiene products I gave all to my brother; the rest my sister would pick up from the county building. I knew the routine—getting up early, preparing for the long ride—I'd seen it every Friday. Only difference was it was my turn. First thing in the morning, I remember being woken for breakfast. I had a lot of things on my mind besides hugging, saying goodbye, and praying with everyone. I remained silent and to myself. I was only allowed to bring with me the Book of Mormon and/or a Bible. Bibles were everywhere. I took the Book of Mormon. Pictures that I had I put a few in the book to bring with me even though I was not supposed to.

As the selected few were called out to be chained wrist to ankles, all kinds of stories started coming to mind, the kinds of stories about how prison was, especially quarantine.

Standing four galleries high, the most talked-about story was people jumping or being thrown from the galleries and dying. I would be lying to say I was not fearful. The county is giving you over to the MDOC, so when they brought us in after going through a series of locked and unlocked doors, we were to be stripped, showerd, and given our prison number, depending on what order you came through the door.

All counties were bringing them in at the same time. It was my turn. I was stripped down. They made me put white powder all over my body as I showered. I did not know what it was, but before I got into the shower, I had to let it set all over my body for a few minutes before I was allowed to wipe it off.

They had to look in my mouth. I had to bend over so they could see if I was carrying something between my butt cheeks—you know, bend over and cough. Finally, after all that, they escorted me to my one-man cell. The only thing I had at that time was my Book of Mormon and pictures of Jade. I laid down and went to sleep.

So for the most part, quarantine was where the MDOC sent inmates to go through a series of text and evaluations for security and classification as to what level an inmate would go. Quarantine was very loud and wide-open, something you would see in a prison movie. People sang, yelled, and talked a lot of trash to correction officers and inmates. I used to love when Cos (corrections officers) tried to talk over the intercom. It was then that every inmate used to yell out swear words and vulgar language that I just found funny.

I was singing to myself in my cell one morning. I thought I was singing low so no one could hear me, but he hit the wall and said I had a very good voice. As distracting and loud quarantine was, I heard him say that his name was Anderson. He loved to sing as well. Since we both had nothing else better to do, we sang songs that we both knew. Anderson being twenty years my senior, it was mostly songs from my time cause I did not know most of the words of his songs.

I thought it best to start learning quarantine and/or prison life to see what I could or could not get away with, meaning the rules of what was expected as an inmate. Although I had eleven years to do before I saw the parole board, I did not want any trouble. Staying out of the way was what I was going to do. I pretty much spent my days walking the yard and talking to Anderson; he asked me to learn some of his songs so that I would sing with him at service. The songs he wrote were not all that bad, so I agreed.

The first time I had my first encounter with a homosexual, I was stalked and did not know it. I was caught with my pants down looking at one of Crissy's pictures. Showers were wide-open, so if one wanted to have personal space, you would have to wait till the other side of the wing went to yard. When I decided to do something, the homosexual walked by and caught me in the act. I was mad as hell 'cause after that, he never left me alone. One day, while sitting in my cell I opened the Book of Mormon that I had. For the most part, I did not put it down till I finished it. It was the first book I read as an adult; I really enjoyed that book. I was still singing with Anderson. We even sang for the church services. At first, I was scared, but it was not that bad. Crissy started writing me more. At first, she was not writing at all. I still could not call home. No one was sending me any money; I was pretty much on my own.

One fine evening, the cell block started rapping Tupac. It was the hard parts; the one or two inmates rapping did not know the words either. I started rapping; shortly after, everyone was listening to only me. That's when I really got into it; eventually, the corrections officer told me to stop. An inmate across the gallery told me for every song that I wrote him (Tupac's), he would give me a pouch of bugler. That was a blessing on time. I had nothing. I knew most of his popular songs word by word as I wrote them. True to his word, he paid me.

I did not like being there; I had no choice I really hated when the homosexual guy tried to always ask to do things with me. Quarantine was not very fun then. Singing with Anderson, later, I saw an inmate being escorted by two officers whom I thought to be a woman inmate. I saw breasts and long blond hair. I found myself waving and saying, "What's up?" The deepest voice turned and said, "Hey." Everyone started laughing at me; I was so embarrassed. I should have known better. Anderson told me it was male that had a sex change, so they had to be separated from general population.

Not long after that, my brother Earnest rode in. He was in a cell across the hall. We did not have yard together; that did not stop us from talking. There was a lot of stuff we had to catch up on, and we did. He saw I had none of the things I should have being in quarantine as long as I was there. Earnest asked me what I needed. My brother proceeded with a store order with everything I wanted and some. Hygiene products, snacks, envelopes—I was very thankful.

For some reason, I really liked shift change in quarantine, third shift to be exact. There was a very beautiful corrections officer that worked. Every night she worked, all the inmates would go crazy. As she and the other officers walked in, inmates would start shaking the bars, yelling, and screaming some of the most vulgar language you could expect coming from the inmates. The first few times, I did feel bad for her. Honestly, it did not take long before I thought it was funny as hell. She seemed surprised the days she worked that they would say those things.

At this point, I was trying to get more into reading and writing. Anderson still was asking me to sing Tupac songs. It was crazy 'cause I would have everyone's attention. I knew it; I did it for them. I really liked that a lot. My time in quarantine was about to come to an end.

Before I left, I needed to get some help putting my appeal in. I did not know anything about law, and I sure as hell wanted to try to get back. Anderson said that if I paid him, he would take care of everything for me even though I had no money coming in I agreed to pay him. I don't know what he did, but I did get my appeal.

CHAPTER FIVE

Bloody Creek

A few days later, I rode out to my first prison, IBC Bethany Creek Correctional Facility, formerly known as Bloody Creek. About a week before I rode in, there was a big knife fight between the whites and the blacks. On the way to the big prison yard, you had to enter this fenced-in cage. This is where I was told shit hit the fan. Inmates from both sides closed the doors and had war within the prison, so that's where the Bloody Creek came from. When I was told I was going there from quarantine, I was scared as hell.

Ionia had all-level facilities. Someone could do his whole prison bit there. Level one was right down the hill, Riverside was down the way—that was a level-two. Max facility was next door to the level one, and then there was MR, which was closed at the time.

Most of those prisoners that were at Bethany Creek came from there. MTU was right next door—that was a level two but ran like a level three. The bus trip was so long; we stopped at every prison, dropping inmates off through Detroit, Jackson, and St. Louis; we even went through Muskegon, Michigan. We finally reached Ionia, where I was dropped off. I came in with about fifteen other inmates. We were stripped to nothing to see if we were trying to bring anything in like drugs or weapons. After nothing was found, we got assigned to the units that we were bunking in, which was two blocks.

It was just like the movies. Everyone new coming in at that time had to go there.

My first bunkie's name was Bill. He was a decent guy. We got along pretty well; mostly, we talked about our cases at the same time, getting to know each other. After I told him about my case, he told me about his. I thought he was clever yet funny at the same time. Bill said he was a roofer. When he got jobs from contractors, he would scope out their homes, wait till no one was home, cut holes in the house, and rob them blind. That is what I liked about being his cellmate. Me just being a silly person, I did not think his situation was funny at all; he was looking at a lot of time. He had gotten in trouble and left his wife. His newborn child really had him hurt; he would pace back and forth, sometimes stopping to beat his head against the steel door. I thought he was crazy at first.

Bill did not mind sharing his food or anything I needed. I still was not receiving any help from back home; times were hard. I was dependent on getting my personal needs met by others within the prison system. Through this process, I was finding myself more deeply depressed. Random thoughts were racing as I mentally beat myself up for being in prison and what I had done to get to this point. I wanted to commit suicide but could not work up the courage to fill this desire, leaving me feeling that my sense of humor was the only thing I had to offer to myself and others. Anything I could use to make people laugh or smile made me smile. So I found myself constantly drawing attention to help keep my spirits up.

We were privileged to go outside three times a day, one hour each period. This included one hour in the dayroom, small yard, and big yard. All the units went to the big yard together. The only problem that I had with the yard system was pending what wing you were locked on. You could have all your yards pretty much back to back all in the morning and be stuck in the cells for the rest of the day.

A good thing about sitting in the cell all day was my cellmate was into the Bible as much as I was. We prayed together, read scripture together, and had services as well. Neither one of us had television at this point; he had ordered his but had not received delivery yet. Since I had no one sending me that kind of money to get my own TV, I just decided to read all the time.

I have been growing my hair for about six months by now, so I was looking for someone to braid it for me. This was how I met Luda. He was my size and looked to be if not my age, just a little younger. I asked him if he would do my hair and told him my situation as far as my income with no help from home was concerned.

He must have thought I was joking upon coming back with some loose cakes from an open box my bunkie (cellmate) had. He made sure that inmates in the hole dayroom seen what I had to offer then they all laughed at me, I was consumed with embarrassment. Felt as though I was becoming the laughingstock amongst all my peers. After they had their good laugh, he told me how hygiene and food worked while being in prison. Since he had a good laugh at my expense, he agreed to do my hair the first time for free. I then asked him would I be able to keep my cakes, and he said no.

Luda, while doing my hair, recommended to me that if I was going to continue growing my hair, I should learn how to do my own hair, and so he offered to teach me. Any time outside my cell that I could watch or learn how to, I learned what I could. Just like anything in life, nothing happens overnight, but I stuck with it.

As time passed, things were picking up with Crissy and I, she was sending cards and letters. It was good in spite of our current situation of not being together. She had gotten a new job, even sent me pictures of her working at her work station. I was very happy for her. When the bills were all paid, she told me she would come to visit me and bring our son. I was also told that I would be getting a TV, which I was really looking forward to; I had not watched TV since the county jail. With all the time I was given, I thought a TV would be form of comfort in my cell.

The worst thing about Bethany Creek was that all the predators had gone there when MTU shut down. I was always getting offers for things, sweets, zoom zooms, wam wams (food), and smokes. I thought they were just people trying to be nice; at the time, I did not know they were predators. I just remember them always looking at me funny and always asking if I was all right.

While on the big yard, one day, Luda introduced me to Red (I can't remember his real name). Red and I became good friends from that day forward. We shared pictures, worked out, and walked the yard every time we came out together; he was good people.

On the day that my bunkie got his TV, he moved to general population. I was not alone too long; the next day I got a bunkie (cellmate). Slim was his name; he too was from Muskegon. I didn't know him. I had gone to school with his sister; I thought that was cool as hell. Slim was really into the Bible and praying. I mean very deep. We got along fine; the only problem that we had between each other was the fact that I smoked and he didn't. It would later cause a problem.

Luda had gotten moved to GP (general population) by now. So when I was on the small yard or in the dayroom I was with Black, I used to work out with him. Black was from Muskegon, Michigan, he was the first person that I had come across with life in prison; he was never going home.

For the most part, he was just someone that I could talk to; he locked right under me. When I was in my cell and had nothing else better to do, I would just yell down the hall and talk to him for a while.

By now, I had been holding out for as long as I could without smoking in our cell. I got to really wanting just few hits of tobacco one night. I told my Bunkey Slim I was going to set by the vent and have a hit. He started yelling at me like I was a child, proclaiming what he would do to me if I did.

While we were bunkies, we did a lot of hands-on contact in the sense we were sizing each other up. The other reason I really didn't believe him was because he proclaimed himself to be a man of God. I truly believed he would do nothing to hurt me. Even with eleven years, I told myself that I was going to stay out of trouble. So I was not going to fight or pick up any weapons for anything or anybody.

I lit the cig by the vent so he wouldn't have to smell it as much. He jumped down off the top bunk and tried to slap it out of my hand, so I pushed him back. That's when he punched me in the face.

34

It had been a long time since I was that mad, but I held back from hitting him back. I just yelled at him.

Black, from downstairs in his cell, was listening to everything the whole time and told me to beat him up. I just lay down; I really felt soft. That night, after not speaking, he told me how sorry he was. He said that as a man of God, he should have never put his hands on me, so I forgave him.

The next day, I was moved to GP unit 500. When I got to my new unit, my bunkie was sleeping. Ty and his three other codefendants were in different units. We had never seen each other, just here and there. My bunkie and his codefendants had robbed a store. In the process, they ended up killing someone that worked there. They were charged with armed robbery and felony murder.

I asked about his case a lot and how he felt about being a part of killing another human being. I thought that was crazy for myself to actually to be in the presence of killers, people that were never going to be with their loved ones again. So I listened as Ty loved to talk. I got a lot of stories out of him. I enjoyed hearing the stories.

I still worked out from time to time, so when I would go to the big yard, I would still see Red. Not long after that, they rode him out. I never seen him again.

CHAPTER SIX

Twin

I started going to the law library a lot, trying to fight my appeal. I did not understand law or what it was that I had to do. Most of the time, I would go to the library because it just seemed like the right thing to do. A large percent of the time, I just sat over there and talked to people. I found out that I had a homeboy (person known from the past) from my hometown. We used to go to the library all the time and have in-depth conversations a lot.

I am from Twin Lake, Michigan, about a half hour outside Muskegon, Michigan, but I was still in Muskegon County. I went to the library every other day, and when I did, I was there with him. I just called him Skee Town.

Correctional officers shaking your cell down was a daily routine; it was a part of the order of prison. Personal shakedowns normally happened every day; everyone hoped for the female officers to do the shakedowns. I remember my first shakedown by a woman very well. I, Skee Town, and a few other inmates that were getting ready to leave the library were all directed to line up. The woman officer grabbed all our private parts. Skee Town went first. He said "Hey hey," standing with his arms out on his tiptoes, then I went next. I could not believe she did that, but I didn't complain. Things just happened anyway.

My hair was continuing to grow out. I still had no knowledge of how to do my own hair. I could not afford to get it done myself. I didn't have conversations with anybody around the unit at the time. Ty introduced me to a guy across the hall. I don't know his real name; he was just known as Old School, or just School.

Normally, I would not just talk to anybody, but Ty said he was pretty cool. He asked me if I was interested in making some money. I asked him what he was talking about. I don't remember the punk's name, but School locked with a homosexual.

I still was learning the prison life. I didn't understand that if you did not have a soft spot for homosexuals, you did not lock with them. If you did, prisoners would start questioning you and spreading rumors behind your back.

Truly I did not know their situation at the time; it did not bother me either. Just as long as no one said anything to me. I forgot the punk's name, so I will just call him Punk. That's what homosexuals were called, Sissy or Punk.

School asked me if I would hold a few gallons of spud juice and make it if he could get the orange juice and sugar. At first, I was like absolutely not; a substance abuse ticket was serious. I was still seeing mental health at the time, trying to get in the med line, not because I needed it—I just wanted to get high and sleep my time away. A substance abuse ticket would stop all of that.

He and Ty promised me that if something were to happen and we were to get caught, they would both take the fall for me and not let me get into any trouble. That was an offer I couldn't refuse. So I told them to let me think about it.

That day, I needed to get my hair done. I saw this new guy around doing hair, so I went and observed him doing hairstyles and cuts. I asked him how much he charged; he told me two dollars. He informed me that my hair was too short at this time, that when it got long enough, he could style and cut for me. Every day after that, when I was not working out, I continued watching Twin do hair so that I could learn. He was my age, maybe one or two years' difference.

I finally got my first job on the yard crew; I got paid between ten to fifteen dollars a month working every day. Sucks, right? It was basically not enough to even take care of myself. Crissy was making about five hundred a week at the job she was working at.

I was trying to get her to help me buy a TV, and she agreed. Bella and Joe must have gotten sick of me asking them for money and complained to her. She said she would buy the TV for me, but she could not send it all at one time. She sent me a fifty-dollar money order, said she would send the rest next week. I did not hear anything else from Crissy for about three weeks to a month; finally, I just spent it. A while later, she sent the rest and told me to get the TV. I was very upset.

Since money wasn't coming in, and I had to take care of my habits. I accepted School's offer reluctantly to hold the Spud juice. I told him if anything was to happen for him and Ty to at least keep their promise. I did not really know School enough to trust him. Ty, I trusted.

I was also very gullible. I would learn a lot of things the hard way. They got me about four or five gallons of orange juice. I put it in my state-issued bag under my locker; it was too big to fit inside my locker. For the next few days, School explained how the process worked to create and assure the recipe was a successful product. He directed me to add water, sugar, bread, and other ingredients needed for a successful recipe. After a few days, it started smelling really bad. It was blowing up. Every hour or so, we would have to what we called burp it. Just around the bag so that it would not erupt.

After about a week or so, I tasted samples of a few bottles. It was the nastiest stuff I ever had drunk. Spud juice is rotten orange juice. I drink it just before entering the big yard. By the time I got out there, I was intoxicated. I really enjoyed my sip.

The next day, my mom came to see me for the first time; we had a good visit. I asked her why she didn't bring Crissy. I had been under the impression that Crissy would be coming.

I had not seen her or my son since I was at the Muskegon County building. I was not going to let that mess up the visit with my mother. We talked about God, the Book of Mormon, and everything that had happened and what was going on back home. I was happy; she informed me that if I did not have enough money to get me a TV by Christmas, then she would get me one. So she left on a very good note. I really love my mom.

When I got back to my cell, I saw how all of Ty's things were gone. I even noticed how the bag with the spud juice was not big anymore. I checked the spud juice bag, and there was nothing there. School sent me a car with a letter telling me the whole story. A car is just a long line of dental floss with pencil at the end of it; the pencils are just for weight. In the letter, he told me everything that happened. He explained that during chow time (dinner), there was an assault on staff. I forgot the officer's name but she was always messing with the inmates, talking bad to them, and always doing shakedowns.

It was known that if they could, officers would pick with the inmates to provoke them to get hit so they could get ninety day off with pay. She picked the right one that day; it almost cost her her life in the process. The inmate hit her so hard that her lungs collapsed, sad that everybody hated that lady. Ty was there when it happened. They told him keep moving, but he laughed and began to mock them. Officers took him to the hole. That's when they came and packed his property and found the spud juice.

While the officer that found the juice did his round, he told me what he had found and that he was going to write the ticket. I told him to ask Ty because it was his. He told me that if I was telling the truth, he would not write the ticket against me.

About a half hour later, the officer came back and said Ty did not accept any responsibility for the spud juice and that he had to write the ticket against me. I was mad. That would be my first of many lessons I would learn—no one to be trusted. What I did not understand Ty was never going home. He had nothing to lose. Why did he not take the fall like we agreed?

Ty was gone I did not want to just locked with anyone. Our Arus was all right; his name was Mr. Cults. During yard I went to proper authority and asked if I could pick my next cellmate (bunkie). He said since I did not get into any trouble and was not a problem around the unit, he would do it for me.

CHAPTER SEVEN

Infringement and Betrayal

Besides the few people that I walked the yard with did not really mess with anybody else. I was still fairly new to the unit the first person I thought about was Twin. We were about the same age, we got along, plus I could learn how to do hair.

So I asked him if he and his bunkie got along, he told me no, so I asked if he would like to be my bunky. He told me that if I could make it possible, he would do it.

I got the move done within the next few days. Besides him not having a TV, everything was going well. We shared stories and pictures. In that short time, he was teaching me how to do hair.

I saw how much money doing hair was bringing in. I needed a way to make money. No one was looking out for me back home. Crissy was still writing and sending cards, but the money stopped all together.

Even though my oldest brother had told me rules I should live by while in prison; one of them was not accepting free stuff from other inmates. I thought at the time Twin was different. I had his back; he had mine. We did everything together after that. We worked out, went to the library, and we even started going to church. We became good friends.

Twin continuously without question ordered every item that I needed from the store; I never even had to ask. I just felt that he was like a friend at home, just looking out for one of his boys.

Power would go out there for days at a time, a few times a week. Those times, I would really start to get to know the real Twin. He told me about how he liked boys and thought that I was sexy. In any normal situation, that would be scary. I felt like Twin was cool and no matter what would respect my boundaries.

A few days after that, I saw Skee Town. I had not seen him much lately. I told him about Twin being homosexual. I told Skee Town that he had cut into me. Skee Town wanted to fight him right then and there. I remember pulling Skee Town back, begging him not to say anything. Skee Town told me locking with Twin, nothing good was going to come from it. I felt like I knew Twin and everything was under control. Skee Town never spoke with me again.

A few days later, Twin asked me if I was interested in trying some pills. I asked him what kind, and his response was pain pills. Fighting the sleep was how I would get high because they made you sleepy. So I agreed. I remember taking the pills. Everything after that was pretty much a blur.

I remember getting up when I heard the doors open. In level four, the Officers controlled the opening and closing of the doors. I jumped up, put my shoes on, and started trying to walk. I then realized that I was stumbling all over the place. I felt as though I was drunk.

I heard someone say that the movement was for their yard. I wanted to go to chow. If it was yard, then I had missed chow, so I grabbed something sweet from Twins's locker. Then I lay back down. I remember waking up. I didn't know what time it was; all I knew was it was dark.

I could only see the light coming from the room cell hallway window and the outside window. Twin was over me, touching me in places he should not have. The pills had taken full effect, leaving me helpless and confused, so I was powerless to his actions. I fell back asleep. The next day, I never said anything to Twin about the incident.

I vowed to never talk about that again. I was very upset at myself. I had let my defense down. I was violated, and I was responsible for this happening to me. I was powerless. I felt that I would not beat him in a fight. Using weapons was out of the question.

Needing someone to talk to, I called home to my mother's house. My mother accepted the call, and we talked. A few of my brothers and sisters were there; I have a total of ten brothers and sisters. Not one of my siblings were sending me money to help me out; it hurt.

I could not accept what I was really upset about. This was not about them not helping me but what had happened to me last night. I could not hold anger back any longer, so I cussed out my big brother. I informed him about how I felt them not being there. I told him if they did not want to help me, I would just get one of these punks to take care of me.

I then proceeded to take my anger out on him. I began yelling at him about a time when I was a child sleeping on the couch in our living room at home. He and one of his friends had come to the house. While my brother was in the back room, I had woken up with my brother's best friend's private part touching my mouth. I had woken up feeling him slapping me in the face with his penis.

I had rolled over and gone back to sleep. The next day, when I told my brother, he had called me a liar and did nothing about it for me. When I was talking to him, he had told me that we would never speak again. At that time, I did not care.

I felt as the world had failed me; there was nothing in the world for me. I was feeling an overwhelming amount of stress. I could not cope or integrate the emotions involved with that experience. All the bad things that I had done I felt were back to kick me in the behind, and it hurt like hell.

I knew I had to get out of that cell with Twin. I started drinking coffee so that I would stay up. I would not let what happened that night ever happen again. Twin had taught me how to braid by now but not good enough to start charging people. I still needed some practice, so that's what I did, everyone that would let me. I did their hair for free.

One day, while I was just coming in from the shower, I found a letter on the floor. Well, seeing the paper on the ground, I did not know it was a letter at the time; that was till I picked it up. The letter was from Candice. This confused me because he was one of the few people that use to let me braid his hair when I was in the process of further learning to braid. Even though I was doing a crappy job, he insisted on paying me.

I just thought that was cool and overlooked anything else. The letter showed his true intentions; he just talked about how much he liked me. If I needed anything, I just had to ask, and it would be mine. Him being overfriendly, I shared the letter to Twin.

By now, the whole yard must have thought that I was Twin's bitch. I can recall a memory of going to the yard that day, and the whole big yard was watching us. I didn't know what was being said behind my back, but whatever it was, everyone knew about it. I had to get away from Twin.

For the most part, the officers there were all right. If you stayed out of their face and out of the way, they did not mess with you. Some you could interact with, and some you could not.

There was a sergeant there that I believed was really cool; his name was Lawder. Sometimes I would push my emergency button just to come out and talk to him. In doing this, I had someone to talk to that couldn't or wouldn't hold stuff against me unlike inmates would.

This could cost me my life. Other prisoners got the wrong idea when inmates talk to the officers for long periods. They thought they were getting told on, which most times was true. At that point, I just didn't care. The only person there I could talk to was the personnel at Mental Health; I was still talking to them.

This gave me the opportunity to acquire pills. Sergeant Lawder was the only one that listened at the time. He pretty much knew everything that was going on with me, everything. He did not say or do anything, knew that he could be trusted. So whenever I needed someone to talk to, I would have him to call me out.

I gave up my privileges of food and personal items needed from Twin. He asked me why I, all of a sudden, was acting standoffish. I explained to Twin that I was trying to do for myself. Before he could say any more, I was called to a visit, and thank God. The whole ordeal with Twin was coming to an end. I should have listened to Skee Town; he had told me nothing good was coming out of being friends with him.

At this time, I had dressed after showering and gone to the Control Center. I saw that my visitor had not been brought in yet, so I sat and patiently watched while I waited. I was hopeful that Crissy and Cameron would come. I knew that more than likely it would only be my mother. It was not though, as Crissy suddenly walked in the room, I had never been so happy to see a loved one in my life, and she looked amazing. We hugged and kissed and spent the whole time talking.

She stayed through the whole visit till they asked her to leave. Earlier, I had tried to get her to leave being concerned about her safety so that she could be on the road, she refused. I told her a portion of what I was going through. Promoters used to call me to fight for them when they needed to fill a card for the night. I had a fighting spirit at home. All the while, she knows me to be tough, so she could not comprehend.

We talked a little more, said our goodbyes, and we kissed. There was something about that kiss that I would never forget; it just was not right.

I went back to my cell and pretty much kept to myself, looking at the wall. Something with Crissy was not right, and I felt it; I needed to know. The next day, when I talked to her over the phone, I sweet-talked her into telling me what the problem was.

When she started crying, I knew this was not going to be good. She told me that she would write a letter and tell me everything. The letter could not come fast enough. This seemed to be the longest I'd waited. The letter disclosed her having sex with four or five different guys since I'd been locked up. Three of the guys I knew; two of them I was really close to. One of them I was with in the county building with Nazer.

I had used to show him pictures of Crissy and her friends. He asked me to hook him up, I refused. What hurt the most was that he told me he would have sex with her when he got home, in a joking matter. I now realized he was serious.

I was sick. I was beyond sick to my stomach. I had never experienced such a hailstorm of pain. All at the same time, I was raging with anger and panicking, feeling a pervasive sense of irritation with what they have both done. This betrayal left me experiencing this deep sense of loss. It was the deepest feeling I had ever experienced inside my mind while raging with anger. A unexplainable sense of loss, a betrayal that hurt more deeply than I had ever experienced. My thoughts were racing, thinking about this and that and what I possibly could do? While overwhelmed with anxiety, I was locked up and incarcerated. For my mental stability, I had to just let it go.

For the next day, I just sat facing toward the wall. My feelings were hurt. Twin continued trying to speak to me. In this moment, I was ignoring him. He said, "Forget you." Forgetting I was ignoring him, I quickly repeated his words back at him.

He jumped off the top bunk, as hard as I ever been hit, he slapped me. Officers did rounds once every half hour. That's if they decided to. I don't know how long we fought, but that was the longest fight I'd ever been in. I fought back as hard as I could. He would put all his weight on top of me on my bunk. He put his knees down on top of my arms and began slapping and punching me in the face. The fight seemed as if it lasted for a very long time.

The desk was made out of bricks and came out of the wall. I remember sitting there, on top of it. In the course of fighting, I ended up there. I just could not go anymore. I had enough. I just sat there with my head down. He was still pushing me; he hit me like three more times in the face. I remember looking over seeing School and the punk's faces. They were in the next cell over.

I assume they were watching us. When he stopped hitting me, he tried to give me a hug, but I pushed him back. I just laid down on the bunk and cried myself to sleep.

Shortly after, I woke up with the urge to use the bathroom. I saw that Twin was sleeping. There was no way that I was going to remain in this room any longer. I wrote a kite (note) for Sargent Lawder to call me out as soon as possible. I waited for the next officer to do his rounds. When I saw him, I did not want to wake up Twin, so I put my hand to my mouth to tell him to be quiet. I gave him the kite, and he walked off.

A few minutes later, my door slid open. I ran down to the sergeant and told him everything. I told him that I refused to go back into that cell. He told me he understood. He said he knew someone from the other side that was a nice guy. His name was Malvin D; everyone called him MD, short for Mad Dog. I had seen him around the unit here and there; we had never spoken to each other.

It really did not matter to me as long as he was not trying anything funny. I could lock with anyone. I started back to my cell to get my things, hoping that Twin would be still sleeping, as I really was not looking forward to facing him. To my surprise, he was.

I sat there on my bunk bed and waited for about a half hour before the door opened. I was told to pack my things to be moved to the other side of the unit. As I woke Twin, he seemed as upset as well as surprised. Twin showed no remorse; he was the cause of whole thing. He kept asking why they said I had to move. I informed him I had been lying in the cell the whole time and did not know. While in a repetitive conversation with him, I continued to pack my property while assuring him that I would get some answers.

As I walked out the door, I was thinking to myself how happy I was that I was out of that cell. I did not have a lot of property so I was quickly getting my belongings. On my way out the door, I told Twin that I would catch him in the big yard. I was gone.

CHAPTER EIGHT

Mad Dog

I walked around the other side of the unit to get to know my new bunkie. In getting to know MD a little, I learned that he had a sleeping disorder. He would be having a conversation with you while he was falling asleep.

MD had been resting for a long time. I was really looking forward to him waking up. I needed his help, I strongly felt he could educate me about the system. Then I could prepare for the sentencing time. I still had to serve.

Upon putting all my property away, I just anxiously sat on my bunk while MD was continuously asking different questions. I assumed MD was analyzing me as he asked to see my photos. He seemed confused that the mother of my child was white.

As with everyone else other than my mom's brothers and sisters, I informed him that I had attended a mostly white school as with my neighborhood.

Truthfully, I was paying more attention to his TV. I was enthusiastic about watching television. I only had one bunkie prior with a television, and it stayed on the Christian channel. I enjoyed seeing something different as I watched the news. The days ahead, I focused on what was going on in the outside world.

Everything else went or stayed normal. I continued to go to church but not like I was before, but when I did, Twin would still sit with me a portion of the time.

No one really cared to go. I was getting used to new guards, inmates, and bunkies; it was a whole process within itself. We also did not eat with general population. I was not getting to the big yard as much; our unit had become the intake unit for all new prisoners.

This was not a problem for me with all the bad things going on in general population. Other inmates felt the same; they had been moving inmates to different units. They would bring our food to us; this did make a lot of sense things were simple for us. We continued to have fights in the unit occasionally, nothing serious.

While on the small yard working out, I was told by an officer to report to my unit and call home. This was not routine. The officer could not tell me a reason for the call. Panic and anxiety swallowed me up. I did not know what was going on.

I returned to my unit to make my call. Crissy answered to inform me that my brother's newborn baby had passed away. My brother was taking it really hard; he called me and asked if I could call home and speak to him. The baby was born while I was in prison, so I did not know what to say.

There was a song by Scarface and Jay-Z called "Can't Be Life." The song referred to loved ones that had lost their child. I called my brother and said to him the same words of the song. I told them how much I loved them and said my goodbyes. Ella informed me they would like me to call more. I proceeded to call every other day.

MD and I were still currently getting to know each other. While in the yard, another inmate had told him that I had locked with a homosexual. My first reaction to his question was to deny this. I claimed I had no idea what he was talking about. For the first time since I was moved in to GP, no one was pushing me to do things I did not want to do. Since I got moved into unit with MD, I felt secure and safe from a lot of different things going on around me.

I told MD I was not homosexual, and I acted really offended. Who would ever say something like that behind my back? I felt a sense that in my reactions, I had overreacted. Nonetheless, I knew he did not believe me.

A few days later, while I was sleeping, MD came in from yard. He calmly proceeded to insinuate that a homosexual was on the yard looking for me. He proclaimed he had told a story about me. While MD proceeded to tell me this, I knew there was not any truth to his story. I almost surrendered the truth. He informed me of his conclusion that he believed me. He would have my back for now on and if anybody said anything about me.

MD and I became really good friends following our conversation. He would let me watch TV sometimes; we always did cook ups, and he always looked out for me. A day came while on the top bunk, MD was sitting on the edge of the bed and fell off. I never understood why he locked up there, knowing he had a sleeping disorder. I must add it was the funniest shit I ever seen.

We informed the sergeant, and he had us switch bunks. MD had weighed at least 250 pounds. I was only about 130 pounds. Moving was all right with me.

It was MD who introduced me into gambling. M.D. used to play tickets, all it was is like the usa today, and sports lineup of the day wrote down on a piece of paper. Upon him showing me how to understand it, it was very simple after that. For example, you had five picks and six picks. You also had what they called Ron Robinson, short for RR, which was a six pick. If you were to put one dollar down on a five pick, you could win fifteen dollars. Whereas if you put one dollar down on a six pick, you could win $21.50. A short and simple explanation: placing a bet on either pick, you win double. If you put five dollars on a five pick, you win $15 five times, $75.

It was football season at the time, I pretended like I was the king of football. I told him whom I thought would win, and he put them down. All the picks came through for him. After that, he was always asking me about who I thought would win. I hated when football season came because that was all he wanted to watch. If it was not Sports Center, it was NFL Live. If it was none of those, it was the games itself.

I did at least get to laugh though, MD would hit his head on the stairs or on the table. Sometimes he would do it back to back. His sleeping disorder was kicking his ass.

I had no money coming in. Occasionally, MD would put in tickets for me. Then I could play, five picks was all I could get. Just like drugs I became addicted, MD was hitting tickets every other week. Some of his hits were coming off my picks, I decided to leave gambling alone, for a while. Deep down, I knew I would play again.

I started doing MD's hair, even though he was capable of paying someone. It was cool—he would look out for me and the practice I needed. The only problem with that was he felt like I had to do his complete head.

This became a problem when I started to feel as though I had to do his hair all the time. When he would ask if I would say no or just not right now, he would turn off his TV. This would infuriate me. I would be persuaded in doing it anyway.

I did not always have soap. I would take showers every other day. MD told me it had to stop. I had to go every day. I understood what he wanted or was trying to say.

He demanded time to himself. MD liked to take off all his clothes when he was in the room—alone of course. He would wait until the lady COs would do rounds and ejaculate. Some wrote tickets, and some did not. Sexual misconduct tickets were not to be played with; this could possibly keep you from going home. I had not been down long enough to be doing that stuff.

I do remember the day when I did not go to the shower with someone I knew or MD. The showers did have cameras, but there are blind spots from the cameras. While taking a shower one day, I saw this guy looking at me funny. I continued talking to some other guy from the rock, so I did not pay any attention to what he was doing. Not paying any attention to my surroundings, one by one, all the guys were gone except me and that weird guy. His name was Woodz. He was a Moor. Between the different religions in prison, I was always warned to watch out for Moorish Americans.

Everyone had left I turned because I heard a shower door slam open. All the stalls had doors. As I was turning, I could see Woodz was standing there all bricked up. Caught off guard, I was speechless and proceeded with haste, washing the soap off to get out of the shower. Before I could get all the way out, he had his hands in my way and was in the stall with me. I tried pushing him off, but he was stronger than me. He had turned me all the way around before I heard other inmates coming up the stairs from the downstairs shower. He moved back. As fast as I could, I wrapped my towel around me and ran as fast as I could to my cell.

MD was still in the shower, so I dried off, put my clothes on, and laid in my bed as I cried myself to sleep. I wanted to kill myself. I lacked physical strength. I would not even stand up for myself; I truly felt like a little bitch. The most thoroughly confused part about it all is that I had no one to confide in. I could not have this discussion with Twin because what he had done to me prior. The only time I seen him was at church. Even though me and MD was all right, I came to the conclusion I could not trust confiding in him. What had happened to me would just give him something to use against me.

MD and I would have disagreements. He would turn the TV off so that I could not watch it. I felt the only one who could understand was the Lord himself. Nobody could understand at home; besides, they were living their own lives. I honestly felt I was dealing with the worst time of my life. Woodz never mentioned what had happened to me, no one else did either, so all was well.

I got called to the control center with regard to my substance abuse ticket. I don't know how; it was dismissed. I was happy as hell. This would not last for long.

While watching a preseason game of football with MD, I believe it was Lions against Bears, preseason game. MD was taking bets from people down the hall. One of the guys' name was Raff. On occasion, I did his hair. Other than that, all I knew about him was that he was never going home. He, just like MD, had life in prison.

Raff and MD were placing bets on the football game. Raff liked the bears; I liked the Lions. Even though I had no money to bet at the time, I saw this as a fast opportunity to get some money. I was not thinking smart though because it was only a preseason game. The Lions did control the game; however, the Bears came back to win.

I bet on ass which is a no-no in prison. Gambling without the means to pay can get you killed, Raff told me when the doors opened it was going down, I was afraid of what could happen to me. When the doors opened and we went into the day room he threatened me and said if I didn't have his money he was going to stab me by nine o'clock. I don't know if MD just wanted to see me sweat as he could have paid the debt, nonetheless none of my other friends had any money to pay either. Raff was a killer and highly respected around the unit so his threats were taken seriously. At the last moment, MD did pay the bill, I learned a valuable lesson as raff and MD pulled me to the side and spoke with me about what I had done, I was told never to borrow or gamble what I could not pay. This time I had a pass as a lesson of doing prison time.

Even though most of the time I continued to gamble, I was able to provide my personal needs. MD and I were getting along very well from the incident with raff, as I owed him from paying that debt he started noticing how much interest I took on his TV. He would make me rub his back while he lay down to watch TV. Perturbed as I was, I did it anyway. I wanted to watch TV that bad; it made me really soft then.

Due to his sleeping disorder, he would quickly fall right to sleep. I would just watch TV. When he moved, I would start rubbing again until he went back to sleep, it was the only way I was able to watch TV. Even though I opposed this agreement, I did not care; I just wanted to watch T.V.

Currently, my life was in full swing. Everyone wanted to know what I was doing and where I would be so they could join me. I was the man. I had a woman, drugs, money, and most of all, respect. In one night, I lost it all. I was now rubbing another man's back to watch TV. It was ironic how my life had changed.

My life was all good just a week ago, when I thought things couldn't get any worse. I called home to speak to my brother Brock. I got more and more bad news. Currently, Ella and Brock were not getting along. While talking to Ella, I was inquiring about my son Cameron. Ella babysat all the time, so I was just asking her if she had seen him lately. She said, "Jerry, you don't know."

I said, "Know what, Ella?" She told me that Labor Day weekend, Crissy had a party; all my old friends were there.

Ella got tired and went home, and my brother had stayed. She proclaimed that when she went to pick Brock up in the morning, the door was not locked.

She went into the bedroom, looking for Crissy; she found him and Crissy in bed together. She had ripped the covers off them, and they had no clothes on. Brock's arms were wrapped around her.

I don't believe I ever had been that sick before. Ella then went on telling me all the other things that I did not know. Crissy had been with other guys. She said that when she saw my brother and Crissy in the bed together, she kicked Crissy's ass.

Feeling the betrayal, I told Ella to put my brother on the phone even though I did not want to speak to him. I knew that what Ella had said was true. I just wanted to see if my brother would be honest with me. While on the phone, he proclaimed what I was saying was not true, that he had no idea what I was referring to. I did not want to even talk anymore.

I was speechless again, overwhelmed with distress. Deep feelings that she was growing distance from me. All I could do was reminisce about the things she told me before I came to prison. She had told me that she would always love me and be here for me. Crissy was my only real link to the world. She would write, send cards, be my eyes and ears.

I knew it would not last long. She was falling off. All I could do was remember the things she told me before I came to prison.

Overwhelmed, with hurt and disappointment, I was overcome with anger, grief, and humiliation.

As I am feeling disengaged, I kept thinking about a dude from quarantine. We had talked on different occasions. He asked, "What are you going to do with that white girl?" I told him nothing, she was not going anywhere. He suggested to me I would see.

I was now coming to an understanding about what he was talking about. I still had never been that sick before. Ella proceeded sharing information I did not know about Crissy.

Without hesitation, Ella informed me about other men that Crissy had intercourse with. I still could not call Crissy at her house so I could confront her with everything that Ella had told me.

Crissy's first response was to deny all accusations. She portrayed Ella as a self-serving liar. When Crissy began crying, I knew that there was truth to what Ella told me. Crissy only could proclaim to me was that she was sorry. Nothing was going right in my life. I was feeling forgotten, abandoned, consumed with a hollow feeling inside me— an emptiness. I felt as if the whole world were swallowing me up. Entangled in a pain of feeling unloved, I could not breathe. Crissy was supposed to be there to make things easier for me, not harder.

Consumed with my life, I began taking pills again whenever the opportunity would arise. Regardless of what it was, I would take them. MD had no problem; he had been getting high with me. We would literally sleep for three, even four, days. The only time we would get out of bed was to go to chow. I felt this was not very fair. We were usually fed in the unit. MD and I were currently buying a lot of spud juice. On occasion, we would make it ourselves.

In the beginning, we began to eat in the unit. It was easier to get juice. One time, I remember half the rock (A wing upper) was making spud juice while getting drunk. The police proceeded to search all inmates and inspect all inmates' units (shake everyone down). MD and I consumed what we could of the spud juice in our cell. The remaining juice, we poured down the toilet drain. Not clear why, but someone down the hall sent their bag of spud juice to us. Accidentally, we proceeded with spilling spud juice all over the floor. Our room smelled of a very strong foul smell of alcohol. After drinking a little spud juice and cleaning the room, it was our turn to get shaken down. MD told me to pour the rest in the toilet. This was someone else's spud juice, not ours.

After, I poured it out the COs took MD, I and a few other guys to the dayroom. I knew there would be repercussions, with regard to the spud juice I had poured out. The inmates inquired about their alcohol they had passed to our cell. I informed them that I had been forced by circumstance to pour it down the drain. They began verbally degrading, humiliating, and insulting me, while threatening to fight me. Feeling a sense of powerlessness, I became outraged. Though frightened by their whole demeanor, I finally developed a strong sense of self-confidence. Against all odds, I stood up for myself and MD.

In an imperious manner, MD informed them that if there was any problem with me, then they had a problem with him. I finally stood up for myself for the first time since I had been in prison, against all odds. I felt my confidence level rising; I was really feeling proud of myself. So out of character, one of the members of the same prison gang gave his word that I was to be left alone. After that, I felt reassured; not one of their members bothered me. The police did not recover any contraband; we were sent back to our cells.

The rest of the evening, I really enjoyed smoking black and mild cigars with MD. MD would put honey on the cigars to make them burn slower. He typically wore button-down shirts unbuttoned. Honey would drip off the cigar, right onto his chest, leg, or stomach. His reaction was the funniest; he was always nodding off. MD would fall asleep using the bathroom. When I would hear "Ouch" really loud, I knew what had happened.

In spite of everything that was going on in my life, I prayed and hoped that God would make things better. I was young then. I blamed everyone but myself for everything that was going on around me. My next visit with my mother, she opened conversation.

We conversed about placing blame and judgment on others and just how equally quick it was to avoid or deny responsibility. I never told her about any negative activity that was going on with me in prison. I just reminded her that when she could to help me get a TV. I expressed how I really wanted and needed it.

She informed that prior to this visit, she had arranged to pick up Crissy and Cameron. Upon arrival to pick them up to come see me, Crissy canceled. This did not surprise me. I really did not talk to her that much anymore. After the ordeal with her and my brother, our relationship was falling apart. My mom told me it was over and that I should move on. I did not want to believe that, though; I was still fixated on the past and what might have been.

CHAPTER NINE

The Break-up

I continued to spend my days as I normally had. Other than that, MD and I started slowing down on consuming pills. Withdrawing in the process, MD and I would have attitudes toward each other. I knew it was some of the side effects. I gave him a break.

Several new prisoners started showing up around the unit. I had been here for a while now. Even though I did not miss it, everyone I did know consumed pills. Twin was moved to another prison. I pretty much was by myself, if not with MD.

The prisons are categorized into different security levels. In Michigan, levels range from one to five. For example, a level one facility houses prisoners who are easier to manage, whereas a level five prison houses prisoners that pose a maximum management problem, are a maximum security risk, or both.

During this process of change, I found out that I had a friend from home there. His name was Tone. I attended the same school with his sister, and we joined the same street gang.

A street gang is an internal organization that claims control over territory. They typically do not accept members unless they live in your neighborhood. Several members know you and will vouch for you. In joining, you would be jumped in. This was a process of initiation where you would fight one or more other members for a certain number of minutes.

What a gang respects most is courage, intelligence, loyalty, and authenticity. What others seem to fail to see in this lifestyle a gang is supposed to genuinely look out for each other and the people in their neighborhood.

It's funny that I say that because I had long given up this lifestyle. The only time I could and would see him was at big yard. We started working out together; our units went the same time.

I had a good idea about how to survive in prison. I definitely knew not to trust no one. I choose my words carefully and hide my emotions. I never repeated what I heard. I was not a snitch, and I never would stare at other inmates. I showed the guards respect as well as any prison employees.

Tone had been in the system for a while. I took the opportunity to learn what I could from him. I did notice that Tone was always with homosexuals. I really did not understand why they came with a lot of drama.

While privately talking to Tone, I inquired about his interest in the homosexuals. He informed me that he was basically their pimp while explaining that they took care of him. Other inmates had told me different stories. I was told that these were his lovers; he was homosexual himself. I did not care. I was not here to judge Tone. I was just happy to have a homeboy, someone around that was from home. I knew if "shit hit the fan," truly he had my back.

I started building my own clientele. More people started having me do their hair. I needed the money. I really liked gambling on sports. I continued to stay away from the poker and card tables. I had seen too many people get hurt and lose too much money. I refused to be one of them.

I can say that I did like the whole idea of making money off people like Tone had managed to do.

The first person that I could try it on came just in time. I can't name him. We will just call him Old School. He was white and way older than me.

I remember him being overly happy on this day while down in the lobby. I saw him looking at me, actually staring at me. We were on our way to church. Before we left, the unit had to get each of their passes signed.

This is when Old School first spoke to me. He mentioned to me that for some time, he had been watching me. I felt a sensation of uneasiness about him; he seemed to be kind of creepy. Regardless, I ignored my gut feeling. I felt the need to hear what he had to say.

As we were walking to church, he asked if he could sit and talk to me there. I did not like the whole idea of this. I did agree I would hear what he had to say.

He repeatedly mentioned how he had been watching me around the unit, that he had a deep desire to get to know me better. He asked me if I was homosexual. I told him no. Though that did not matter to him he was looking for a friend. He mentioned his desire to write me a letter; I agreed to read it.

I saw this as an opportunity to make some money. Tone had successfully done this in his unit when he was here.

The next day, upon receiving and reading his letter, I was stunned. I had never read a letter as disturbing as this letter in my life. Old School's letter consisted of fifteen pages long, if not longer. His fantasies were beyond my comprehension; he wanted me to perform the worst, most sadistic sexual acts on him. Old School asked that I become his sex partner.

His sexual fantasies had paired sex with violence. He had a deviant desire to feel nothing more than as a sex object, himself. In his fantasies, he suppressed strong desires for me while proclaiming he wanted to be the receptive partner. He wanted to have anal intercourse with me. During this course of action, he desired for me to humiliate him. I was to forcefully anally penetrate him, while at the same time punch him in the back of the head. I was to cause him much suffering and pain and laugh while performing this act. This was only one of his sexual gratification acts that was dependent on suffering physical pain and humiliation. He was a masochist, I was shaking from my foundation as this was new to me, someone feeling or wanting this gratification. I was sick to my stomach and refused.

Old School proclaimed he had a family company that made films. If I moved to his cell, became his bunkie and lover, and performed heinous acts, in return, he would give me all the money that he received every month. If I moved to his cell and performed heinous acts on him. I needed and desired his money but could not come to those terms of agreement. Not long after his offer, I took his letters, and soon after, he rode out to a different prison.

I took notice that it had been a while since I had heard from Crissy. I had written and tried to call numerous times. We needed to talk; however, I never received a response from her. Approximately three months had passed, when I received a letter.

She stressed her need to break off the relationship with me. She desired to see other men. Crissy had sent me a Dear John letter; receiving this deeply hurt. I felt a lonely feeling of emptiness and sorrow, deeply feeling Crissy's betrayal. We had talked about this while I was still at the county jail. I wholeheartedly asked her not to leave me for someone else. I asked that if she was not going to be with me through this whole process then to leave me now. She had proclaimed to me that she felt our relationship was like broken glass and all the pieces could not be put back together.

She pronounced that she was going to get married to Larry. This was a friend of mine back home. He, his twin brother, and I used to sell drugs together. This had me livid, hearing that Larry had just shot somebody five times and almost killed him for nothing. Outside of the fact that I might have been jealous because he was a friend from home but also I didn't want those types of people around my son.

She informed me that she had called the prison (IBC) and requested the removal of her name on my list so that she could put it on Larry's. Then she had the audacity to tell me that she was not going to stop writing. She wanted my son and I to stay in touch, to stop any confusion so he could understand I was his father. She would not allow anyone else to take my place.

Honestly, her words meant nothing to me. She had already betrayed me, been unfaithful, disregarded opportunities to visit me, and now she wanted to let me get to know and be with my son.

I was overwhelmed with emotions of jealousy while shaking in anger. I hung up the phone and went to my room. I then proceeded to rip all the cards and letters I had received from her. I was feeling alone, upset with a deep rage, while disappointed to be out of this relationship. Beyond disappointed, there was nothing I could do. I was incarcerated at the time. I came to the sense of realization that life goes on.

Truthfully, when I was told the truth about Crissy, I had sat in denial. I always expected her to be there for me. I came to the realization I had to accept the truth. She had fallen out of love with me. I felt empty. I was holding on to my memories while feeling a deep sense of loneliness and loss.

I understood she had the right to move forward. Crissy didn't enter our relationship with an understanding that I would be locked up. I knew it would be hard keeping our relationship alive across the boundaries of these prison walls. I could not be angry about her choice. From the time Crissy had our baby up until I got locked up, I was unfaithful. I realized that she had stayed by my side and that every problem we had in our relationship was a result of my actions.

Crissy is, and was, a beautiful person, the best woman that I had ever been with. While I was in my cell, I was overwhelmed with anger and disappointment yet understanding. I looked at all those ripped-up letters and cards around me. I was able to reach a moment of acceptance of myself. Of my choices, my responsibility, understanding, and peace. I began having thoughts about all that stuff I had time to do.

As time progressed, mostly life remained the same. MD and I got along, Tone and I continued to work out. At this time, I was still making a minimum amount of money from doing hair. I was feeling disappointment I hadn't heard from home. Everyone on the block told me that this was to be expected.

I met a religious set and started doing his hair. His name was Beal. This is what I knew him by. He was older than me, one thing I knew was that he paid very well to have his hair done. Beal made an offer that I really had to put thought into. One could say even to consider it would be selling my soul.

This also went against everything I believed. he presented his proposal with a knowledge of how bad he thought I wanted a TV he offered that along with a big radio and a store bag full of anything I wanted worth up to $200 under conditions of agreement to do a sexual act I wanted a TV bad even found myself giving it thought which was crazy considering I was not that way besides when Twin had violated me, I had never have done anything like this prior in my life, but there I was, considering his offer. I ended up taking him up on it. As bad as this is, that's how bad felt the need for a TV. At this time, I was willing to sell my soul. The plan was to depart to the shower at the same time and both enter the blind spot. As we did enter the shower, we began removing our clothes together.

We played a lot at first. I thought that he was joking. I did not hear his tone. While preparing for what we had come to do, I suddenly felt the urge to change my mind. I stopped taking off my clothes.

I pronounced that I changed my mind. I tried to put my clothes back on. Beal did not see things that way, though. In a stern, threatening way, he said that I was going to finish what I had begun.

I was fearful. I knew that it would be painful. My thoughts racing about how much respect I already lost amongst my peers. I was considering the fact that no one respected me. I could not bear the thought of hearing any more rumors.

I was about to get a TV along with all the other items that was agreed upon. In this last moment, I knew how strongly I desired respect more. I looked at his face. I could see that he was serious.

I was currently in the mop room trapped upstairs with Beal with no one around. If I yelled, no one would hear me, with a very slim possibility of inmates in their cells. I knew that my only possible way out was going to have to fight.

He was much stronger and bigger than me. Regardless, the inevitable was that he would overpower me. I didn't have a chance. The worst feeling in the world was when he did have me turned all the way around, overpowering me. I tried to keep faith in my strength. I worked out. I was now going to make raping me impossible for him to do. He needed at least a hand to guide himself. I was not going to give him a chance.

My reality became a nightmare. That's when everything changed for the worst. Woodz walked into the shower room. I was all by myself. I never felt so alone in my life. MD would've helped me; however, I could not get to him nor him to me. Twin had ridden out a long time ago. Tone was in a hole at a different unit. Woodz grabbed me. I put up a good fight. I tried to call out, yell; no one came to my aid. I was beyond exhausted. While fighting both of them what seemed to be a long period. I was pushed down to the ground. Woodz put me into the blind spot shower and left me, but no one was around.

When I came to, I fully understood what had taken place. I went to my cell broken, thinking what would be my next step. I thought to myself, *How could I be mad for putting myself into that situation?* All I had to show for it was the bag of tobacco he had given me.

I have not talked about that since. No one ever asked about it either. I did speak with Sergeant Lawder on occasion. When we needed to talk we did.

I just wanted to stay in this unit for as long as I possibly could. I was told by him that he would keep me there long as he could.

Officer Powers wanted to move us out of the unit. I did not want to go back to general population; changes had been starting to take place. Level four facility was becoming a lower level, from a four to a level three, only meant that pending, what side you were on. The difference was depending on how much time you could spend not being locked down.

It was a different story for MD; he would be leaving very soon. We did not know if we would ever become cellmates again. We proceeded to get drunk and enjoy each other's company for the next few days, that we would be cellmates. Just as we believed shortly after he was told to move to a different unit.

Discontented by his move, I was feeling a heavy emptiness with his departure. I was disappointed and sad. Other than his control issues within our unit, everything else about him was great. I was very thankful to have shared a cell with MD. One of his great characteristics I admired was he always showed me loyalty. I would share with him my deepest secrets, and confide in him for advice. He didn't share any of my business or threaten to use against me. He was my trusted friend and confident. When others called me derogatory names such as "faggot" or "fuck boy." He always stood up for me. MD didn't care if I was wrong; he always had my back. I felt a deep love and respect for MD. In truth, I did not know how I would manage without him.

* * *

Time still moved on. I did not get any bunkies for a while. They did move an inmate next door from the hole; his name was Steve B. We quickly became good friends. He saw that I had no TV. All he did was sleep, so he gave me his for a few days. All I had was a broken-down tape player MD had left me.

Steven just took that. At that point in time, this was the first time that I could lie in my own bunk and watch TV, which was all I ever really wanted, to be left alone and watch TV. Bethany Creek had all-night power, so I watched TV nonstop every day till I had to give it back.

I didn't even know him like that for him to risk giving me his stuff; that act alone had gained me a lot of respect for him. I tried to get him moved over to be my cellmate. It did not work. Soon, we were all about to be moved out of the unit, which would be our next move. I just asked Sergeant to make sure that when we had to move, to make sure Steven and I went to the same unit to have each other's back.

True to his word, he did just that. We were moved next door to five block. We were the last ones to leave that unit as that particular unit was being turned into the hole. He let me stay there as long as he could. I did not know if I would see Sergeant again, but I knew as long as I was there, he would check on me.

CHAPTER TEN

General Population

It was dark going to five block, which was the hours most inmates were on lockdown, so I knew not many inmates would be out and about. Steven was locked in the same hall, which was very cool; we would see each other a lot.

My new cellmate was in the shower from how the room looked. Just guessing, he was a Muslim from the things I had seen posted on the wall. When he walked into the room, he told me his name was GP. The first thing that he asked me was if I was homosexual. That had me thinking someone was trying to do their homework or someone had told him something false about me. He did tell me that's what someone did tell him. I was not surprised. I told him no, and he took my word for it. We talked for a while, getting to know each other. I learned that he was younger than me, doing a life bit without parole for murder. He was a part of a robbery gone bad; someone had gotten killed. He told me what happened the night of his case as I told him about mine.

He started asking me about the books I was reading, considering I did not have a TV. At that point, I had the Book of Mormon and the Bible. I had read the Book of Mormon and was using the Bible as a footnote for higher understanding.

That is when he went on this big tirade about Allah and how he was one, not how Christians make God one with Jesus, going on with this and that. I felt that I was strong in my faith and the things I believed in, so I did start to rebuke or stand up for what I believe in. Something about the things he was saying I could not stop thinking about. I had been told to watch out for funny Muslims from the beginning of the process coming into the system.

I also knew that being a Muslim also brought some form of protection if need be, being another positive. He said he was a Sunni Muslim. I liked that idea, as I did think they stood apart from the other Muslims. Whites could be Muslims, and that was all right.

As the days went by, I would be talking to Steven, telling him everything that was told to me; of course, he was trying to hear none of it at first. Truth is, I did not want to do it alone. Steven was my right-hand man at the time I had become a Sunni Muslim, and I wanted him to be one as well. After telling him the things GP told me, he finally became one and took the vow to become a Sunni Muslim.

When we made—better yet, took—our vows to be Muslims, we had to pick our Muslim names; I became Raheem and Steven became Rakeeb. After we got our turns, we were introduced to all the Muslim brothers. This was a beginning for me because now I was protected. No one was going to mess with me anymore.

I took my studies seriously. I read every day. I learned the English prayer first. Then I learned the Arabic version. I was praying all times a day, sometimes six and eight. I really started to 100 percent believe in what I was doing. The brotherhood was good to me. I always had something to eat and someone to talk to.

Every day on the big yard, all the brothers would meet. The Sunnies were on, on part of the yard. The Mobits and Malatics and the nation of Islam had there corners of the yard as well. Sometimes while everyone was meeting, people would have to stand post to watch our backs. It was better to be safe than sorry. I was not messed with like I was before I joined to be a Muslim. And I loved that. I thought to myself if I would had done this when I first came into prison, then I would be telling a whole different story.

My mother came to see me and did not understand why I became Muslim. But she also did not question it. I was thankful for that because I know that if she had questioned it, then I would have second-guessed myself. She only told me that she knew that the Book of Mormon was the way. When Mom came to see me, we pretty much just talked about old times and about how she just wanted me to come home.

I was not seeing much of Tone anymore. I was seeing MD until he got moved over to the unit that I did not go to yard with. Truthfully, all that did not bother me though. I had a whole new group of friends that would stand up for me and put their lives on the line if need be. And I loved that.

I remember going to my first *Juma* (Friday service); that's when I heard the Imam (our leader) speak for the first time. Very powerful brother—I can honestly say that to this day I've never been moved by anyone like I have with him There was power behind his words. He looked everyone right in the eye when he spoke. I loved him for that.

I started getting to know more brothers from around the unit. There were two Muslim brothers that locked next door to me and my bunky. One day, while coming back from the chow hall, we were all having a group discussion.

I really wasn't paying attention to what was said or the importance of the conversation. I took the other brother's side that locked next door to us. GP took it very personally.

When we walked into the room, I walked in first, not thinking anything of it. As soon as I turned around, GP was on me and had me grabbed up held in a position where there was nothing I could do.

He told me if I ever took anyone's side over him, he would kill me. From the look in his eyes, I could tell that he was telling the truth. As strong as I was when Ick did that, I felt his power and strength. He later told me he was sorry and would not do that again.

What was done was done and I was not going to stay in that cell, if he would act like that over nothing, there was no telling how he would act if we had a real altercation.

I did put in for a move, and shortly after I was moved, I moved with Rakeeb, my best friend at the time. All we did was play. I was having the best time of my prison term for the first time in a long time. It felt like I could have my guard down.

As close as we were, we really did not know each other, so we took the time to do just that, speaking about your past lives and how much time we had to do.

Rakeeb was facing a simple assault and battery one to five. He had it made coming straight from quarantine. He was sent to a camp closest to home where he caught to many tickets and was sent to level four. That's not good, but he seemed to not care.

He told me about his family, and I told him the same about mine. We used to get *so* bored in that cell. We would make balls out of paper, sit back on the bed, put the trash can next to the door, and see who would make the most. The catch was that every ball was worth five or ten slaps to the face and/or chest. Rakeeb was white and would bruise easy, so we would have to take breaks for him to heal. If the corrections officers would have seen the marks, we could have gotten into trouble. These were the kind of things we did, I guess. more importantly, Rakeeb taught me how to play chess. I remember him showing me how to set up the pieces and how they moved, from there he said I had to learn the strategy as I very impatiently slapped the board of the table. Only to pick it up and set it up again, that was how I learned to play chess.

After being his cellmate for a while, I found that I was nothing but becoming what's described as a Friday Muslim. Rakeeb never did prayer or studied. He just watched TV and played around. All the time, I loved him like a brother, all the same never passing judgment. I did know that he joined mostly to make me happy, and I was thankful for that alone.

Rakeeb had a homeboy next door to our cell. His name was Q. He was like me when he came to prison. He prayed all day, only went to church, and only did the godly stuff. He had a bully for a cellmate. The old man that was his cellmate used to have him in the corner of the room, making him stay in the bed. I guess you could say old school controlled the room.

Rakeeb used to get into their fights all the time, which was how I saw he had heart. I used to have to calm Rakeeb down all the time. They would be screaming to each other from door to door, saying what they were going to do to each other, and a few times after the doors opened for showers or chow lines it almost went down like that.

About Rakeeb though—where I was weak, he showed strength. That showed me a lot. Me and Q started talking a lot, getting to know each other better. I started doing his hair.

I learned later that he had a robbery charge. They gave him seventeen years.

Q also knew Ick, my old bunkie. One day, while going to lunch, we were all going to jump Q's bunkie. I really did not want to have anything to do with it, but I was just going with the flow. Truth be told, I had protection with the Sunni Muslims. I also had to put in my work as well.

Things worked itself out though. We never did have to beat up Q's bunkie. Not long after that, Q moved to a different cell with one of his homeboys. Buck was his name; he had life in prison for murder. He was cool as hell. Buck and Q were fun to be around so I started working out with them. One evening while in the big yard, someone tried to stab Q. His coat with a book in it saved his life

Q did not want to do anything to get back, and I did not blame him the fact of the matter, was that if he did nothing to get back, someone else would see that and take it as weakness. That was what Buck and others were telling Q. They talked him into stabbing the guy back, and he did while at lunch the next day.

Me and Rakeeb, Ick, Q, and Buck went to the chow with each other. When Q saw him, he was to take care of them 'cause if a fight broke out in the chow hall that you go to the hole and level five fighting in the chow hall is considered inciting a riot, so we sat there till the guy left. When he did, we went with him. We stayed back while Q went and took care of him. Q hit him two times in the back before the police came.

The knife was slid close to me. I did not know what to do with it, so I passed it to Rakeeb, and he gave it to Ick.

Since they could did not pin a weapon at the fight, Q only got charged with a fight. He was taken to the hole.

We all could have got into trouble for that. I could've gotten a weapon charge. Q could have gotten an assault with weapon.

I found myself in the middle of four other people's drama I did not know. I had to step back, and I did.

After not getting into trouble for the part we played in the incident, I got really deep into my religion. I found myself feeling good, studying hard, reading and praying five times a day.

I found more time outside of my cell by working on the yard crew. Even though we used to cut grass all the time, I still enjoyed myself 'cause I was getting out little more. Ramadan (the Muslim fast) was coming, so I was doing everything to get myself ready for that.

Ramadan was where a Muslim ate after the sun went down till the sun came up, but we also prayed and studied all day. I had every intention of holding the fast and staying diligent, but things don't always work out that way

Rakeeb wanted to play all day, every day. I can say that at first everything went well, but after the first few days, I saw how things was going to be, so after a while, I just gave up the fast.

Outside of my cell, I still worked out with Buck and worked on the yard crew. Candice had started working on the yard crew as well, but I did not hold anything against him for what he had done.

We started talking again. I found that Candice was all right. Besides, when I felt that he was trying to hit on me. I just felt all that was just a part of the everyday thing (prison) by now though.

I found myself talking to Candice a lot more, walking the yard, telling him about my problems. He was a good listener, so I was telling him about a lot of stuff that was going on back home. Rakeeb and I were starting to have our differences.

I was trying to take the oath of being a Muslim very seriously, whereas he was more lax with his attitude toward it.

So I decided to go talk to my counselor about a possible transfer to a different prison. Guilty by association, I had made a very bad name for myself at Bethany Creek. Our arus was a good man from what I could tell. Anytime that I wanted to talk to him, he was not funny and always let me into his office even though he did not have to.

He went over my prisoner file with me and told me that if I gave him a continued time frame that we agreed upon with good behavior, he would transfer me to a different prison.

While there in his office, I asked to be moved to a different cell, although Rakeeb would not like that. I just felt that I needed to do what was best for me. I needed an environment where I could take my studies a bit more seriously.

Besides, we had got caught playing with steel rods from the TVs by third shift officers. They wanted to take us to the hole, but we talked our way out of it. We did have contraband. They took it and left us alone. A week or so later, the move was done. Rakeeb was hurt, but I tried to tell him about how I was taking the oath for real and wanted to be in a place where I could study and really learn the deen.

My new bunkie's name was Joe. He did not have a TV, so I just let him watch mine while I read and studied; he respected my space.

When I did any of my five prayers, this being my first Ramadan, I was taking it quite seriously. I had to read daily, curb my thoughts, not eat or drink in the daytime, focusing all my thoughts and efforts toward Allah.

Things were going well for me and my new cellmate. We got along well. He did what he did, which was watch TV and I did my studies. I found myself looking over to watch my TV with my cellmate a few times. All he watched was the country station. Up till that point, I really did not have anything against country music, but some of the stuff he was listening to I really liked. I mean the music was really good, so I started liking country music.

Besides, I was not really talking to anyone from home except my mother. She was still coming to see me as much as she could, which was about once a month. Truth was, those visits were the only thing really keeping me sane or from going crazy.

Coming off one of the visits, I was asked to do a big cook up for the brothers. While my back was turned, cooking in the day room, I was robbed for everything except my TV. At first, I thought it was my cellmate, which made things weird between us, till I found out later it was not. Nonetheless I wanted out of that cell. After talking to the arus and letting him know what had happened, he agreed to another move and sent me to Sam's cell.

CHAPTER ELEVEN

Carson City

I did not know Sam from the street, but I knew him from around the prison, and what I did know of him was pretty good news. Him being down to earth and all, we started talking about our cases. I found out that Sam was in prison for murder. Life without parole.

He told me that he had beef with some guy around from where he was taken the up street. They set an ambush. One gunman at the street light and two more gunmen up the street. His girl saw what was happening before the ambush could happen; she started shooting out the window while he drove. The gunmen were too much.

My bunkie did make it, only to find his girlfriend lying slack in the seat. When he felt it was safe, he pulled over to find her dead. Later, he retaliated and was found guilty of murder.

Telling stories and getting to know each other better was pretty much how our days went. I still talked with Candice when I worked the yard crew. I was thinking we were friends and everything was cool until one night while working yard crew while putting all our tools up and everybody was off, getting ready to go back enjoying cake and pop. Candice pressed me for sexual favors. I begged him to stop; he overpowered me. I did not yell out. I just stood there. Finally, I acted like someone was coming, and he stopped. That was the final straw for me.

Although I did not tell anyone, I pressed Cut to ride me out to a different prison. Even though he told me that he did put in the transfer, I did not believe him, so every time I saw him, he told me to just be cool.

After pressing him for about three months, I was finally told to pack up. I was riding out. I had been at Bethany Creek for two years. That was, hands down, two of the hardest years of my life. I made it out without getting killed.

Bethany Creek is a level four prison facility, and as your level drops, the time is supposed to get easier, and as I packed my things, I said my goodbyes to some of the homeboys like Rakeeb, Buck, Ick, and some of the brotherhood.

I started to realize that while lying in my bunk how prison was for real and that if I did not start doing something very differently, then it was very possible that I could die in prison. Either by my own hands (killing myself) because let's face it—I could not do nine more years like I did the first two.

Or someone else was going to kill me for some reason. I had in my head that I would not fight, only if I necessarily had to, and no matter what, I would never use a knife. I realized that if I wanted the way that I did time and how people messed with me, then I should reconsider using deadly force when people tested me.

I rode out the next day to Carson City Prison Pac. It was not a prison nowhere near as bad as Bethany Creek, so I was happy to hear that.

I rode in and saw some people that I had seen around at Bethany Creek. I did not know personally where there, so I did not know if they would say anything about what they knew about what had happened to me. In prison, names and titles just stick, so if I was looked at as being soft, weak, or homosexual, that's what everyone was going to think of me, so I tried to just tsay low-key.

First, my bunkie was named One Eye. After talking and getting to know him better, I was told that he had lost his eye while being shot by the police. One Eye and I became cool, and for the most part, One Eye took me under his wing.

He introduced me to his circle of friends, and everything was working itself out for me.

I got into the weight pit and started working out. Another good thing about Carson City was that we were out two more hours than Bethany Creek. We only went out two hours at Bethany Creek, whereas at Carson City, we were out four hours.

From telling stories with my bunkie Ick from Bethany Creek, I was meeting people from his stories, so after talking with them, I found that I had more people to talk with.

I still did go to services as a Sunni Muslim. I got to know different brothers. By now, I was not doing it for bettering of self. I was in it for the name, for the sake of "protection."

My relationship with Crissy was not going so well, yet we still talked. Mostly through letters. I could not get to know anyone from back home to send me money, and that was pretty much the cause of our fights. I was trying to see my son, and Crissy would not bring him up.

I finally got on the yard crew and started braiding hair. I wasn't making a lot of money, and it was getting me by. For the most part, things stayed like that for a while, and then I was told to move to the unit next door. Carson City had a level 4, level 2, and level 1. The level 4 only had two units, and that's where I went. For the most part, long-term prisoners pick who they want to be their bunkies. I did not know at the time, but I had been chosen. My new bunkie's name was Sag, short for Saginaw. Sag was about six feet, 250 pounds.

Even though I had been working out, I was still only 5'4". With clothes on, I was 130 pounds. He had already did his homework on me because the first thing that he asked me is if I was homosexual. I told him that I was not, but I can tell by the look on his face that he did not believe me anyway. For the most part, we did not talk much. I did me, and he did him.

One of the benefits of being his bunkie was that he had a lot of money from playing poker. So I started off doing his hair, and he would pay me and smoke with me. Even though I had what little money I did from doing hair, it was not enough to eat off of and support a smoking habit.

Through Sag, I was introduced to one of my homeboys from home. I just called him Ski-town. Ski-town played poker as well, so my bunkie and him were cool, so Ski would always check in on me here and there.

Sag would be still trying to talk about or ask me about being homosexual even though I told him I was not. So one night during movie night, we were watching the movie *Cabin Fever*. I started watching it but had some things on my mind, so I cut off my TV and just lay there.

I don't know if my bunkie really thought that I was sleeping or if he just did not give a care and was going to try his luck, but as I lay there, I started to feel the bed move. At first, I thought nothing of it, but then they called count, and during count, it stopped. Shortly after, the bed moving started again. I went to jump off the top bunk to use the bathroom, but when I looked down, I saw my bunkie with all his clothes off, not even trying to hide it, jacking off. I acted like I did not see anything and asked him, "Did the CO go by yet?"

Anybody else probably would have been fighting my bunkie, and maybe I should have for him being disrespectful, but I did nothing. The next day, I was eager to get out and tell my other homeboys in hope that someone would do something for me, but they all laughed and thought it was funny.

By lunch word got back to my bunkie about what I was going around telling people. My bunkie came in the room while I was cleaning the floor and asked me why I was going around telling people he was jacking off while I was in there. I guess you could say that he did not want people to know that he liked boys. Even though everybody already knew what mattered was that if people did not talk about it out loud, then it was not relevant.

I don't know where I mustered the strength from, but I said, "Well, you did do it." I don't think that I was scared; I just knew that if it came down to fighting, he would probably win with all the odds in his favor. He did not fight me though. He told me that he did not care where I went, but I had to get out there without telling the CO why (I did not want to be labeled a snitch).

So I packed my things, walked down to the officer's desk, and told them that I was refusing to lock down and that I needed to either move to the hole or a different cell. For some odd reason, I was scared of going to the hole, so I felt really good when I was told that I would be going back next door from where I came from.

I went to Double-O cell. I know of Double-O from Bethany Creek. He said that he remembered me, but that was about it. I had personally seen him put other people on blast for things that people did not want other people to know about, and that was one of my fears. That he knew something about me and would tell people.

Double-O was down to earth. We talked here and there but nothing about our personal lives. We did braid each other's hair, and that was cool. I was able to do my own, but why do it when I could have someone else?

I started hanging out with Double-O's circle of friends because most of them I knew from around the unit, but I also was doing their hair, so it was pretty much everyone was cool with everyone. City was one. We was all right. He was from Detroit; that's why we called him City.

Twin was another one. I was more on better speaking terms with Twin I used to always make him laugh, so that's what he always wanted me to do.

Then there was Shorty 40. Shorty 40 was as tall as me and my weight, so for once, it was all right not being the smallest of the crew.

When I was not doing one of their heads, we all were either working out or just hanging out, telling stories. That's how I found out that all of them had life in prison and was never going home. For the most part, about six months, everything seemed all right. I was building friendships and bonds, and when I was not with my bunkie and his circle of friends, I was with the Sunni Muslim brothers. By now, I was moreover considered what we liked to call them Friday Muslims because that was the only time that I did my prayers. Nonetheless, none of the brothers would let anything happen to me.

My relationships from back home was pretty much no better. I did not speak to anyone but my mom, and she continued to see me once a month. Any word that I got from the street was pretty much from her.

She used to try to get Crissy to come up with her, but she never would. She used to tell me about times when she used to go out and they tried to get Crissy to come visit, only to find my son around the house with Crissy nowhere to be found.

I knew that she was drinking a lot, partying, and liking the fast life, but all I could do was try to put it out of my head as best I could.

One day, while working out in the big yard, I came in the cell to find out that I been robbed for all my personal things. When the doors were opened, and if a person was not there to watch the doors, then your cell was subject to get robbed. And mine did.

People talk, though, and I quickly found out who had hit me. I was not surprised to have gotten hit, but I was caught off guard by who had hit me. It was Twin and two of his close friends, who were all tight with us. Also, when I went to ask them about it, they all wanted to fight, so there was nothing I could do. Not only did I not want to fight but also, even if I did, there were too many of them, so I just let it drop.

I could not go tell 'cause I would be a snitch, and they have no love or respect in prison for snitches. So I lay back.

People considered soft, weak, or homosexual in prison are pretty much considered prey. For some reason, I did not want to understand that from everything that happened to me.

On my free time, I was still braiding hair to get things that I needed. My next-door neighbor asked me to do his hair in a style that would take a few days, but he would pay me well. His name was Chi. That's not his real name, just what he went by.

Our yard was limited for how long we got outside our cells. The next few days, I did his hair talking to him. He also had a life without parole prison term, unlike most of the older prisoners. I liked Chi. He was cool as hell, told me that he was not guilty and would be going home one day.

Candice was still around. He would walk the yard with me while I did my yard crew job. Another was that I had a few dollars coming in working a state pay job from when I first came to prison, so from me being down with all these people, it was going downhill. They felt they could do things to me and nothing would happen.

That was when a homeboy rode in that I had known from the streets. DR was what we called him.

DR and I played with each other as kids, so there was no question that we had each other's back.

I was still mentally messed up from getting robbed by some of the people that I thought was closest to me. My cellmate, Double-O saw that, gave me a lock to keep my locker locked up, and introduced me to Mo, short for Mobit. Truthfully, I did not like them very much. Reason being, most of them were predators of the weak and people they could prey on. Old School was different. I could tell that by his demeanor and the way he carried himself. Him being from the streets of LA most likely had something to do with that.

From there on out, I pretty much was his shadow. All we did was work out every day and tell old stories about our lives. He really did not mess with anyone but, for whatever reason, took a liking to me.

One day, while we were working, I was called to the officer station and was told I was up for a new job, which was to become a wheelchair pusher or handicapped caretaker. My job would consist of taking the ones that need help pushing them in a wheelchair, or walking them to the yard. I took the job and moved in with my new cellmate. Blind is what they called him. Just before he caught his case, he as a grown man lost his eyesight. He told me that he was caught with a brick of cocaine and got life in prison.

My job was to basically take him everywhere he needed to go in the prison facility. I had to write his letters and read him his letters. I walked him to and from the yard and chow hall. Besides that, I was getting paid fifty to seventy-five dollars a month in prison—that's a lot of money.

I was going to save the money that I made from work and eat off braiding hair, and that's what I did.

A Sunni brother that I seen around playing pool or working out next to me. We never talked, but one day, I introduced myself to him. He told me his name was Nasir day by day. We started talking more and getting to know each other better.

I found out that he had been having problems with this girl from back home and that things were not going to get any better. He had a fresh seventeen years in prison to do so. I knew that the only thing I could or would do was be an ear to listen, and that's what I did.

I pretty much had a set daily routine that I kept too. If I was not working out with MO and DR, then I was doing hair. My bunkie did not need me to be with him during yard. All I had to do was take him out and bring him back in one day.

My cellmate stayed in our cell while I worked out with my old bunkie, One Eye. One of his homeboys robbed me, he came to my cell and told Blind that I had him sent to come to get combs there. Instead of getting combs, he was getting my food and hygiene.

My cellmate had no clue 'cause he would listen to the TV with headphones. When yard was over, I went to my room to find that everything that I had worth money was gone. Food, hygiene, and headphones. I had gotten things took from me too many times.

By now, I wanted to take action. My cellmate could not see being blind in all but he could see the shadow or the silhouette of a person. He told me that he felt bad for letting the inmate come into the cell. He said that he could describe the shadow of the guy to the corrections officer. Him going to the corrections officer would be considered snitching.

I thought it was better him than me, but I wanted to get some of my stuff back. So I pushed the button to get the correction officers to open the cell door. We walked to the officer's station, and my cellmate told what had happened. He told the correction officers that the shadow looked like the only inmates that could, which was porters. So after telling the corrections officer, it was narrowed down to one guy. After locking down, the corrections officers came to my door. About half an hour later, others came and told me that they had found most of my things. I was pretty happy about that. I went about my time as if nothing happened.

DR my homeboy was down for whatever. He told me that if I fought, no matter what, he had my back. I did not want to fight. I wanted him to go work out with me, but every time I went in there, it seemed that he was either mad at me or did not talk to me. I acted like I did not understand, but I did know where he was coming from.

He felt like I had gotten robbed one too many times, and it was time that I stood up for myself and fight. Truly, I was ready to stand up for myself. We even talked about plans on how I was going to do what I needed to do when they came down to get down. I would not act. I went one day to work out with the MO. He looked at me and said, "Don't you got something that need to be taken care of? Don't come back around till it is," which meant that if I was not going to fight, then I had to stay away from him. We never talked again. I still worked out with DR. Herein there, but he was no mo'.

I started working out with Black. Black was blind. He was 6 feet, 225 pounds. Bald head was black as hell, but he was strong, so I started doing pushups and pullups with him. Black had life in prison. We never really talked about what we were imprisoned for; our conversations were more about prison stuff.

By now, I was starting to get tired of Blind. Black bunkie complained about his cellmates, so we talked about switching. I did not think it would go further than that, so I really gave it no thought after that. Nonetheless, we met every other day and built an all-right friendship,

I also, in my free time, spent a lot of time with my Muslim brother Nazer. We played pool a lot, he use to tell me about problems that he was having with his girl back home. For the most part, I was just someone for him to talk to. He told me that it would not be surprising if his girlfriend left him. He told me that he did not know how he would be able to move on. In a sense, I understood because I felt the same way about Crissy.

As time went by, the more and more that our relationship grew apart, my feelings were less prone to be hurt. At times, I would call Ella. She would tell me things like that Crissy was doing, like asking her to babysit only to bring men home to sleep with that whole thing, about not letting my feelings be hurt, which would go out the window.

Nazier told me he would be going to the level two side of the facility. I was very happy for him.

I had been working out, building my bond with Black for a while, when he brought up the issue about cell change. He wanted me to become his bunky, his new assistant, his cellmate to take my place, and my cellmate to take his basic trade, and that happened a lot.

We all went to the corrections officers and asked for the change to be done. The next day, I was told to pack up for the switch. I only had to move my things across the hall.

After closing the door. I started unpacking my things, while Black lay on the bed and talked. He started asking for sexual favors, to do this and wanted to do that. I knew that things would not work out, so I went to the door, pressed the button for them to open the door, and I walked out. I had not been in there for fifteen minutes. I walked to the officers' station and told them that I refused to stay there. I told them that I was being pressed for sex.

My new cellmate name was Richard, forty-six years old. We never talked about our crimes. Other than that, he seemed all right. He was not blind or had to be pushed in a wheelchair, but by now I was all right with the unit officers, so they let me keep my pay.

I stopped talking to Black. I had nothing personal against him. I just did not want to be a part of what he wanted me to be a part of.

Two months after Nazier went to the level two side, the alarms went off and the whole prison went on lockdown. Once a month they did this, my thoughts were like everyone else, though it was a routine shakedown, after about two hours into the emergency count time, that's when one of the officers from my unit came by my cell door and told me Nazier committed suicide. I was told he barred the cell door so that the officer and his cellmate couldn't enter easily. He had taken a razor and slit his wrists, the inner part of his thighs and the side of his neck until he bled to death.

I did not believe that Nazier was suicidal. He told me that when we used to talk about problems he was having back home with his girlfriend, that was all I knew. I was later told that Nazier's girlfriend had left him and he did not want to live without her.

I guess what he told me was true. About a month or so later, I was told to pack my bags. I was transferred to the level two side of the facility. My heart had dropped, I was excited. Level four and level two was a big difference. I still would be doing time with lifers, people never going home from prison. But the rules were a lot better.

In level 2, you had a key to the cell, I was able to be out all day. I packed my things and moved to seven hundred block. I received my keys, went to my room and unpacked my things.

My new cellmate's name was Country. He was from down south, I don't remember much about him, but for the most part we got along well. He was all right.

I had saved all my money from working as a handicapped aid from level 4, so the first thing I did was order all the things that I wanted like shoes, boots, coat, socks, underwear, sweatpants, and a sweatshirt. I was feeling pretty good.

After not being there long, my bunkie Country got into a fight in the yard. I got a new bunkie in, Pops from Grand Rapids, who was kinda a cool cat. Pops was older, so I really loved hearing his stories. He was doing time for domestic violence.

Pop's thought he was a pimp. Pops and I became thick as thieves. I told him over time, more about myself and home.

By now, my relationship with Crissy was very bad. At times she went six months or longer without writing to me. I started thinking about pushing her away altogether. At times, I wanted to hurt her feelings like she was hurting me, so I would not write my son for holidays or his birthdays, which made us fight even more.

In prison, things don't stay peaceful for long. They were sending Muslims and a different religious set to services on the same day, right down the hall from each other.

I was hearing a lot of noise. People were talking louder, than they normally were, so I went down the hallway to see what was going on, I got to the door where the mo-bits were having service.

I watched my home boy Ski Town beating up a chaplain; I could not believe my eyes. The chaplain is considered a preacher on the outside.

The chaplain must have pressed the alarm to call the corrections officers they came from everywhere. The first correction officers jumped on Ski Town's back. Ski Town flipped him off his back and started hitting him. Ski Town was about 6 feet, 225 pounds and in good shape, so it took about three or four officers to get him down and under control. After they took him away, I thought to myself that it would be a long time before I see him again, if not ever. Hitting a correction officer was a whole different case. It was sad to watch my own boy go out like that, but now I'd been in prison for almost three years, so I was starting to get used to people coming and going in and out my life.

I pretty much did what I normally did, workout, play pool, or chess in my free time. One day while working out with pops an inmate asked me to braid his hair. i still did it to make money, so I saw no reason to say no. We set it up to do later. I found him in the yard later that day, did his hair, and went about my day. Later, he gave me a door call to tell me that he did not like the way it looked. He wanted it redone. I tried to make everyone happy that I deal with so reluctantly I agreed, even though there was nothing wrong. He wanted me to do it right then and there, but I was in the middle of doing someone else's hair when he approached me.

So I told him that I would give him a door call as soon as I was done. He had already paid me and was not willing to wait for ten minutes. He told me to go get his money.

I told him as soon as I got done doing what I was doing, I would go get it. That was not what he wanted to hear as I turned to walk back in the unit, he punched me on the side of my neck, no officers had seen what happened.

I told him that I was going to get it. I was pissed. I wanted to fight. I felt 'cause he was a lot bigger than me, I had no chance.

I went to my room and picked up the closest thing to a knife that I could find. It was a pen with a steel point, in that moment I saw in my head the whole situation play out what I wanted to do. I had been pushed around my whole life. Thus far, I had not put any work in. And I understood that if I wanted respect, this was the way to go, but something was holding me back.

I put the pen down. I took out my locker key that was given me earlier, went, and took his goods to him. I felt like a coward.

My mom came to see me a few days later. My mom always could make me smile, and I've always been able to express things to her that I could with no one else. I told her that I really did want to try to move closer to home so that her ride would not be so long. I told her that I would be putting the transfer, and I did. Three days later, I was told to pack my things. I was moving to a different prison shortly after. At this point in time, I'd been down for three years.

I spent as much time as I could with Pops. I told all my Muslim brothers and everyone else that I cared for goodbye, not knowing if I would see them again.

I knew that I would always remember them when I put in a request to go closer to home in muskegon. When I got on the bus the next day, I was told that I would be going to MTU, a.k.a. the punk prison, a.k.a. gladiator school. Everyone in the MDOC knew about MTU. MTU is one of the worst prisons in the MDOC.

At any given time in the MDOC, there could be about fifty to forty prisons in the state of Michigan. MTU was in the top five worst, and there were stabbings, fights, gang rapes, suicides, and deaths. It was bad. My heart sank the whole way to add insult to injury.

CHAPTER TWELVE

Gladiator School, MTU

We rode through muskegon to pick up some other prisoners. MTU was a level 2 on paper but was run and operated like a level four prison. Either way, I was going to have to become stronger and start to find myself or I was going to be in a world of trouble

MTU looked like a college campus when we got there. It was dark when we arrived. It was so crowded there that as soon as we got there, we had to go to the hole and be in confinement.

It was summer time, so it was hot as hell and stuffy. A cell that was made to hold one, was holding me and another inmate.

My new cell mate came from Carson City with me. I did not know him from the yard, but I did see him around here and there. His name was Tone. I had found out that Tone had been down for eleven years, but other than that, we did not talk a lot. Even though we had done nothing wrong, we were locked into our cells at night; I did not like that at all.

It took me back to being in level 4.

We had only one big yard that alternated with the TV room and workout room, so that was the only time we were allowed to get out besides that was chowtime. I started seeing how the prison was run and operated.

Every time someone was brought to the hole, they shut down the whole unit and yard. Being that there were a lot of altercations and fights, they were shutting down the whole compound at least twenty to thirty times a day from fights, stabbings, and assaults on staff. It was definitely out of control. Eventually, after pressing for a move out of the hole, I was told to pack my things.

I was going B unit, my cellmate was going to be my bunkey over there. Even though we did not speak much, I was starting to want a different cell mate. Tone was not bad; we just did the same which made it hard to get into the system. We both like to stay in the cell and have personal time.

I did not like to leave as he did not, each unit had different accommodations as far as, bathroom and dealing with your personal hygiene. Some had bathrooms directly in the room, and some were down the hall. Every time I needed to use the bathroom I would tell him. He used to get mad or rush back to the cell. Sometimes before I could even take care of what I needed to get taken care of. I knew that we would not be bunkies long.

One good thing about being here was that my sister's baby daddy was there. I knew him well from the street. We started pretty much hanging out in all our free time. We started catching up on old times. He told me about how he started using my name when he got pulled over by the police; after I had gotten locked up. I told him that was funny because I had gotten arrested while in prison at Bethany Creek for someone using my name that I did not know about. That pissed me off.

Things were going to be well. I worried about that when I got home. The most important thing was that I knew I had someone who had my back, and he was someone I knew from the streets. I started seeing how everyone was grouped up according to where they were from. Detroit with Detroit guys, Saginaw with Sainaw, Flint with Flint, and so on. And of course you had different religious groups. I personally started going services again just in case I need any support. Will was a Sunni as well, so that worked out. There were a lot of Muskegon homeboys there, but I was from Twin Lakes on the outskirts, so I knew no one. But to everyone else, I am considered from Muskegon.

I talked to my mom and told her where they had sent me. She was disappointed. Like always, she said that we would get through this. She told me that my brother was going to court for something to do with Crissy.

For the most part, we did not talk at all. After talking to my mom and trying to get out of her what she knew, she told me my brother had been partying with Crissy and her roommate Amy. Amy was very young, and he was older than her. I was told that night he beat Amy up and put a gun to Amy and Crissy. My mom gave me his address and told me to write him. But I never did.

Not long after, Crissy wrote me a letter and told me that she was seeing someone named Larry. I knew Larry from the street, so I was very upset about that. I told Crissy that if she was going to see other people, don't see my friends. I felt that she was trying to hurt my feelings, trying to get back for some of the things I had done when I was at home.

Will and I did our thing. We chilled out, worked out, and pretty much were inseparable.

I started talking with other people from around the unit. One day, in the day room, I saw some Detroit boys gambling. So I made my way to the table and put my bet. I won; I beat the guy named Kid. Kid was in prison for armed robbery. His brother was in a different unit; that was all I knew about Kid.

I felt that I could make some money and move on. It started at five dollars a win. It got to the point we were betting tables and clothes. By the time our arms started hurting, I won fifteen dollars, a tape, and a pair of brand-new sweatpants. I was given the tape and told I would get the rest later.

I understood that was a nice way of getting it how I lived basically he wasn't going to pay me, which means I left it alone, of course.

I told him that if he liked basketball, we could play game by game and bet on those. At this point in time, I'm not lying to you, I was almost willing to do anything to get out of the prison to a different one during the NBA playoffs.

Kid went team by team and made our bets, and we paid each other. The next day, a few days into the gambling, we bet, and he won ten dollars, I had a call out where I had to leave the unit before I could pay him his money. So I asked my bunkie Tone to pass his bag over to him. When the doors broke, when I got back to my cell I was told by my bunkie that while he was handing Kid the money, the correction officers had seen what they were doing and confiscated the money.

Simple process that happens all the time, and they were going to give the money back. Kid said that I still needed to pay him, but I said no to wait till they gave me the ten dollars back.

I did not think it was something that we would fight about. Kid wanted to fight, and he took it like I was telling him to get it how he lived.

I was told by other inmates, when it was yard time it was going down. I took the opportunity to leave that prison. Although I feared going to the hole, and did not want to go as there were stabbing and fights every day. Another fear was them trying to get me to tell, and I did not want to be labeled a rat or snitch. I was going to try to shoot my shot.

I went into my unit counselor office and asked to speak with him. I sat down and told him I was feared for my life and wanted to refuse lockdown. He told me that it did not work like that I had to give him more information.

By now, the yard was open, and inmates started coming by the office, looking into the window, seeing me in there. I heard them saying, "He's in there. He's telling, it was." After being in his office for ten minutes, the phone rang, my counselor picked up the phone and was told by the corrections officers downstairs that Kid was with his bunkie and caught redhanded robbing me. Even though that was bad, I took it and ran with it. I was asked to point out Kid and his bunkie's faces in a photo lineup. I acted like I didn't know how the people that wanted to inflict harm on me. I could not do the photo line, but I did see their faces, both him and his cellmate.

They locked down the unit, took me out the back door, and handcuffed Kid in his cellmate to the hole. My bunkie Tone went to the hole as well.

I had never been in a hole; I don't know why I was so scared of the whole experience. I think that I just did not want to be alone. I did not want to be at that prison any longer. Besides, I knew that if I came back out of the hole, me and Kid were going to fight. I knew that if I had held strong and stayed in the hole, then eventually, they would ride me out. They took all of my clothes and gave me a one-piece jumpsuit that hugged me like a dress. It was cold, and all I did was look at the wall. The deputy warden was not going to come back around till next Thursday, so I had a whole week till I would know if I would be riding out.

A few days into my stay, I started hearing this inmate next door always yelling and talking loudly. I don't remember how we started talking. One thing led to another, and I learned that his name was Shorty from Muskegon and in prison for life for murder. I started telling him I was from Muskegon, Twin Lakes. He told me that he knew people from Twin Lakes. They used to come visit him.

I asked him what their names were. It's very small, you know—everyone knows everyone, and he told me "May." I could not believe it 'cause that was my mother. He then told me his aunt's name, and I knew who she was. I knew, okay? She was my mom's best friend, so I knew that he was telling the truth. We talked and got to know each other better, right there through the vine.

I told him what I was in the hole for and that I was trying to leave that prison. He told me not to do it that way. It would travel with me and be good that I should come out the hole. He would help me deal with whatever.

He told me to think about it. Meanwhile, I sat back with nothing to do, when I was not talking to Shorty, I was pretty much looking at the wall. I did catch the book cart one day.

Mind you that up to this point in my life or prison term, the only book that I had ever read through and through was the book of Mormon.

I needed something to occupy my mind and time. When the cart got to my cell, my options were few so I picked the book that had the best cover, which was a fantasy book about demons. I read that book and lost myself within it.

I started getting mail from my sister, Daisha. She told me that as long as she could, she would help me out. Then, shorty told me to tell the deputy warden that everything was over between me and those guys that I would like to move to a unit with my Muskegon boys even though I did not know any of them. He assured me. He would pass word ahead of me so I would be not messed with or harmed.

A few days later, I did see the deputy warden. I told him that everything was a misunderstanding and that I was ready to come out of the hole. I requested to be moved to a unit. If that was all right, they told me the move would be done, and later that day, I was told to pack my things. I was going to be on the other side of the facility.

The deputy warden was letting out Kid as well. I did not know that my old bunkie Tone had gone to a different unit. After packing my things I went to the event. I did not know they were on their way to the yard, and I walked straight out. I just walked around for the most part. We did not have the same yard time so I did not see anyone from the unit, which is good because everyone had labeled me a snitch; that did concern me. As I did laugh, I started to realize that I would not be seen will any longer unless it was some special event or was called out where we were able to meet up.

I went running at the basketball, which bumped my head. I was deep in my thoughts. As I looked up, Kid was running after the ball as well. He saw me and I saw him; we just stood there. Looking at each other, he told me that he knew what I did. He pulled out a paper with the written statement from me saying that I knew that they stole from me. He told me that he was not going to tell anybody. He needed his tapes back, which I had.

Before we went to the hole, we let each other use each other's tapes; plus, I still owed him ten dollars, which the police had taken from me the day we all went to the hole. He asked me about that too. I felt that all that was over, but he did not listen when I told him that

I was not going to pay. He said that next big yard would not be till tomorrow; it was going down.

Honestly, I really gave it no thought. I felt that I would just avoid him. We would see each other if I went to the big yard. I felt that I would just not go to the yard.

I went back to my cell to see my new bunkie; his name was Walt. He was Mexican. We really did not talk at all, basically seeing who each other was.

I went to the day room and found some Muskegon homeboys that I did not know, and they did not know me, but we did have mutual friends, so I started to get to know them. I knew a few homeboys; one was named Col Jack. He was cousins with a close friend of mine, so he was family; that's how we became cool. His bunkie, Black, was from Muskegon as well. They were inseparable. I liked Black. He made me laugh. He was funny, made me laugh all the time.

I found another home boy from Muskegon; he liked boys. To each his own. But too much came with that so I stayed away from him. His boyfriend was one of the biggest inmates in the unit; people called him Cox.

I talked to him one day just sitting around the unit and found him to be cool; it was a prison for young people for the most part. They started to move older people to the prison to try to settle it down to create balance. The administration felt that mixing the old with the young would bring peace, but it had the opposite effect. They started stabbing and killing each other.

They broke up the yard, made different units go to different yards and made the older prisoners move to their own unit.

Some, like Cox, stayed with the young ones and did not move. I always enjoyed having conversations with Cox. Although he was openly homosexual, everybody respected him. He told me that he was in prison for murder. Never going home. He expressed that someone had. Hurt one of his family members and he retaliated. In the process upon being arrested, instead of getting caught, he was about to have a shoot-out with the police. His grandmother embraced him, told him not to, he turned himself in.

For the most part, I did avoid the big yard. I knew that doing that would only last so long, and I was right.

One day I was in the day room when an inmate from Detroit walked up to me and said. He was getting his homeboys together ready for war and that I couldn't run forever. Either come out the unit or they were coming in.

It just so happened that while the inmate was telling me this, one of my homeboys was right there and already knew what was going down his name was Smoke.

I don't know how words spread on the compound about fights. So I was not surprised that he knew. I was mind blown that he came to my aid.

He told kids homeboy that next yard. We would be there and ready for whatever. He told me that his name was Smoke. He knew without telling me what was going down, that he had my back along with most of the Muskegon homeboys that he had told to come to the next big yard. He said that we had to stand together and not look weak.

I did not even know this person, but I was like, "Yeah, you are right."

And so later that day, just before the big yard, I packed all my things, just in case the worst scenario played out. I did not know what was going to happen; I was just going to be there. As we walked to the big yards, you could tell there was something about to go down.

I was actually surprised to see how many Muskegon homeboys were out there. In truth, most of them I'd never met or seen. With forty or so of my boys at my back, Kid stood on the opposite side of me with at least sixty Detroit homeboys with him, who looked just as ready as we were.

Kid asked me for his belongings. I refused and ask for my belongings, to which he said, "Fuck it, it's going down." I knew that Kid or his brother had a knife, but my homeboys did too. I refused to carry or use one, walking to the further back side of the prison yard to fight.

It was Cox who saved the day. He said, "Kid, I know you. Bullet, I know you. You give him his things, you give him your things, and this is over with." And it was so.

The next day, we exchanged goods. It was over. Later, I thanked Cox for what he had done for me. He had singlehandedly stopped what could have been an all-out war over a few dollars.

I soon found that Smoke was pretty much the leader of the homeboys. Whether right or wrong, he was not going to let no one get over on no one from home. I respected that about him. Since he had been in the unit for a while, I asked him if he knew anybody that would be a good cellmate. He told me he did not. My cellmate at the time was not on bad terms, but we both did not care to live with each other.

One day, while I was in the big yard, I was told to come in and pack my things. I was being moved. Even though I really did not care to be cellmates with Walt, I was comfortable. We had an understanding.

So till I found someone I trusted, I did not want to move. I went to my unit counselor and asked why he had moved me without me asking. He told me that the move was done and there was nothing that he could do now, but he told me that he owed me a move, that when I found a bunkie that I wanted, he would do the move.

I walked to the other cell to find my new cellmate was very young. He said he was eighteen. I just called him young one—he was all right, just funny as hell, but I knew off the top that he was no one that I could be with long term.

My brothers and I started talking a lot more. It was around the time that he came back to prison. They had found him guilty. My sister was writing me a lot as well. She was the only one sending me money and helping me out when she could.

Crissy and I pretty much stopped talking. When she would talk, she would talk about how happy she was that she would be getting married soon. I acted as if it did not hurt, but truthfully, it did not. Long after, I found that the guy she was planning on marrying had shot a person five times and was fighting the case of attempted murder.

The reason Crissy had stopped talking and why we fought so much was I knew Larry's lifestyle. He was into drugs, carried guns, a gangbanger, and lived a reckless lifestyle. I did not want my son to be subject to that. I just prayed that when he got a sentence, he would go to the prison I was at because I knew that it would go down even though I had a knucklehead for a cellmate.

I started to get into a rhythm. I found steady people to be around. By now, Shorty got out of the hole. He did not come to a unit where I was at because the inmate that he had gotten into an altercation with was in the unit. It was all good, though, cause all the beef was over. Honestly, I still wish that I would have still refused to lock down and left that prison facility. At least one or more times a day, the unit was getting locked down just 'cause of fights, stabbings, people getting hit with locks and socks. I pretty much stayed out of the way. There were a lot of Aryan nations there. What surprised me was the loyalty that they have for each other on top of the fact they stood in their beliefs. Although I had my indifferent thoughts about that, I respect how they stood for what they believed in and they moved with it.

The Grand Rapid boys were pretty deep as well. I had gotten introduced to one of them by the name of Chet. I knew some Chet's from back home, so I knew some of his family. It was not long before we were cool. I had seen how Chet carried himself around the unit. Although he was young, people respected him.

Young Kat, my homeboy, stood up for himself and the things that he believed in. I've seen him fight and he use to handle himself very well.

After a while, we had basically become inseparable. He saw in me what others did not. He was a good judge of character, even though I hardly stood up for myself. I was a good fighter. I just refused to in prison, but I knew that if it went down and it got thick, then I had his back and he had mine. He was another inmate that I got introduced to that I became cool with.

But now, I had gotten to meet a few people around the unit; I was doing their hair. Dre was one of them. He was from Lansing, in prison for selling dope. We clicked right on. I started telling him about my personal life; he started telling me about his. We talked a lot. I found that I could have an average conversation that I normally could not have with anyone else, so we kicked it a lot and talked.

I finally got a job as a porter, working around the unit and cleaning. I would get paid to carry things for other inmates. Food, hygiene, products, TVs—whatever you needed to get from A to B. I swear to God I did not like the job. There was a guy named Butler. I hated him; he took his job way too seriously. This correctional officer was the kind you would not want to get on his bad side I feared him using his power in the wrong way.

Being able to be out a lot did have its advantages and disadvantages. I've seen gang fights, in the showers is where most fights went down one day while going to the shower I walked into what felt like something of bad vibes as I walked in four other inmates were watching another inmate in the shower I knew what was going down as I seen it was the homosexual everyone was watching I walked out.

I remember days like that at Bethany Creek. I had learned that if you did not want any trouble, mind your own business and stay out of the way. I learned those were the golden rules of prison, and I followed them.

My first altercation came unexpectedly. I was sitting in my cell and another inmate that I had seen around the unit, Kzoo, asked me for some paper that I had. The ones I use to write in my daily journal at the time. I told him yes. As I use the paper to write my daily journal in, I thought better to keep. The folders intact and told him no. He suddenly said, "bring your ass to the shower, let's fight!" Startled about what he said, I asked, "what did he mean 'bring my punk ass to the shower'?" It was going down between me and him and truth be told I was far from scared, it was more over shocking how he cut into me and his approach.

I tried to tell him that I would give him regular paper from the store. He wanted to fight flat out at first. He walked off just pissed. I gave it thought. Five minutes later, he's back at the door again. "Bitch come to the shower," he told me.

From working as a porter, I had seen it firsthand, what happens in the shower. I began, "I refuse to go." It made me look soft. I was still trying to avoid fight at all cost if possible. Being that I was led to that prison, that's the last impression that I needed for people to portray. Although I could fight, I tried to avoid it. I tried to avoid fighting at all costs.

One morning while sleeping, I woke up to Butler kicking in my door, yelling about getting my ass up for work, so I quit. I was not going to be disrespected, even as an inmate. Certain rules apply. I got up and ran to Rush's office, who was our unit counselor.

I complained about Butler's actions and asked to be traded, and they allowed it. They let me go to a different job. Since I had read that first book in the hole I started going over to the library a lot. There was something about reading. I had to keep reading; it was amazing, I started reading romance novels a lot. Being lonely, that's all I could read.

The only time that I would get to see my sister's baby daddy was when I was going to service, so I made sure I went to service all the time.

I was not talking to anyone from home besides my sister, Dashia, and my brother. Other than that, I kept to myself. As far as people from home were concerned, I had been hanging out with Smoke for the most part. He was the leader of all the homeboys that would fight with me I owed him for what he did for me when I first came to this facility.

So for the most part, I paid my respects and paid my dues, so I had the homeboys there at all times. That's just how things were in prison. Personally, it was more of a respect thing because Smoke was into things that I wasn't into like robbing people and fighting people, those things that I just did not stand for, which was his business.

He was into a lot of BS around the unit. Although I still dealt with him—I had to for the support if something went down—I had to keep an arms distance away to avoid any other problems.

I liked playing chess around the unit. I was very good. One day, while I was playing chess with Chet when Smoke called me into the day room and said that he wanted to talk with me, so I went to see what he had to say. He asked me if I was homosexual. I told him no. I asked him, "Where did you get that from?"

He said that someone that had been in prison with me said I was. He would take my word for the truth. I knew that no matter what I said, Smoke would not believe me. I also knew that he was only asking to hold something over my head—leverage, so to speak.

This was the first time that I had gotten a taste of Smoke's bad intention. And I knew that I definitely had to deal with him a certain way. I told him that I was not homosexual and had not done anything of that nature.

I could have been honest with Smoke and share some of my experiences with him from Bethany Creek, but again I knew that he was only trying to hold something over my head.

I was not getting along with my young bunkie, so I requested a move again. I was moved next to the officer's station with Gale. Gale and I were pretty cool. Well, he was funny. He told me about his home and his girl. I can't recall what he was in prison for, but we got along; that was all that mattered to me.

One day, while I was in the big yard, there was a race fight in the unit. I thank God I was not in the unit; most of my friends were fighting on both sides.

The same goes hand in hand as in the nation of Islam or any kind of Muslim nation. The Aryan nation was a flag under which white people could follow and be protected, and that's just what it was. So I knew multiple people whom I believed or thought were not racist, but upon coming to prison, they needed protection. The fastest and best way was to join some form of gang or religious set Aryan nation was for the most part the only brother hood that only white people could join as most did. Meanwhile, Smoke and his cellmate Ron from Grand Rapids were the leaders from the Black side Ron was 6'3 235 pounds mostly muscle.

The Aryan nation had some strong members as well their strength came from their numbers. I was told that the leader of the Aryan brotherhood was given to Smoke. A problem may have even got the better of him had not Ron been there to save him.

I thought that was funny. No one talked about it to Smoke face-to-face, about him losing that fight, but it was talked about. The good thing was that no one told the corrections officers that there had been a beef or misunderstanding, and it was let go. Also, everybody got away with it.

Just like being home, summers were the worst in prison. When it got hot out, that's when people started acting strange. I don't know why, but that's when a lot of different altercations happen.

After that, my bunkie Gal got into a fight. I was surprised because he was subtle and kept to himself. He got caught and went to the hole. I felt bad for him.

They moved a guy from Kalamazoo into my cell, I was kind of upset because I really did not get along with him. I had seen him watching me move around the unit and felt he had bad intentions. Everyone called him slim. He was tall a lanky guy. He had bark and no bite. We did talk here and there I just did not trust him so for the most part I kept my distance.

I started seeing a trend wherein people were hanging themselves. The MTU prison facility had a high suicide rate. I guess, hanging from the bars at the door was the theme. Most of the guys that were hanging themselves, I did not know any of them. We would just wake up in the morning and someone had hung themselves, just one after the other.

I did not know what to think. I had lost one of my Muslim brothers to hanging, so I knew the pain of that. One evening I found myself playing chess with Chet and Dre, a guy that I personally did not know asked to play and we let him after winning and talking trash he wanted to gamble. Normally, I would not but since I was caught up in the moment I agreed we decided to keep it low it was three dollars a game after I beat him it went up double. I stopped playing and told him to pay up. We continued to play. But I felt since I didn't know him, he needed to pay what he owed, and then we could continue from there. He went in and got what he owed.

Against my better judgment, I played again. It was not too long I had him right back to the same amount he owed, and so I stopped playing. This time, I could see that his whole demeanor had changed. He was very upset I would assume he was dealing with mixed feelings in the heat of his own anger. He laughed at me and started talking shit. He told me to get paid.

Basically, get it how I live, which means if I was going to fight he was going to fight with me. If not, he wasn't paying me. Fight for it or leave it alone. I knew that if I let it go, that I would have no respect. Everyone would just walk all over me. I see it happen not only to myself but others as well. I had a choice to make. I was sick of being walked all over, treated like a piece of crap.

At this point, in my prison sentence, I still had almost seven years to go. I needed to make a name for myself. I needed to make a stance. The guy was a lot bigger than me but I felt I was stronger. I told him to come to my cell since it was right by the phone in the hallway, even though mine was next to the officer's desk. We waited. They did rounds upon the hour, and we timed it. He came in a rush.

He backed me up to the desk, but I had his hair, punching him in the face while on top of the desk. I remember looking up and seeing someone coming through the door as I was fighting, it was Hazel that called me to the shower to fight. He was from Kalamazoo, just like Slim. His approach was to help if it was Slim. Upon seeing that it was not Slim, he backed out the door. I had been fighting long enough, so after overpowering him, pushing him off me, I held his head down by his hair, still punching him in the face. He said, "All right, all right, I quit. I will give you your money."

I stopped swinging to let him up he turned to leave while I let my guard down, he turned around and sucker-punched me in the face. For a moment, I was discombobulated. By the time I came to, he had gotten a few good hits in. I picked him up, slammed him, and started the same process again, punching him in the body in the face till he cried for mercy again.

This time, I was very watchful of his movement as I picked him up and told him to get out and get my money as I was pushing him out by the time we came out of the cell, everyone was talking to the guy. That I was fighting tried to give me a hug, saying that it was all good and a good fight.

I did not trust him enough to get that close, so I walked around him and told him to give me the rest of my money. He told me that 'cause we fought, he was not going to pay. I said, "We're going to fight again."

Our unit was called to the chow hall for dinner. And so we formalized. In walked, everyone was discussing what had took place back at the unit. More importantly, they wanted to know if it was over and it wasn't. I wanted my money, I was out for blood I was feeling myself as I was questioned and asked the whole way to the chow hall what happen.

Everyone knew that there was going to be a fight. By the time I made it to the unit, it was to the full capacity. I walked in and waited for the guy to come in there. In truth, I was starting to regret fighting while that was a weakness. I felt like if I did, not everyone would walk all over me. I was in a zone, and besides, I had a stage to show that I could fight and very well. The guy came with his Detroit friends some were mutual friends of mine. I said, "We don't have to do this. You could just give me my money that you owed me."

He said, "No, we squared off for the second round." I punched him and knocked him back the day room, quietly watched as it unfolded, I put my back to the wall and tried to slam him, upon which I had all control. He was big, but could not fight.

I heard Smoke yell to stop trying to pick him up and punch him. I did some way, somehow, he got me in a choke hold that I slipped out of quickly. I punched him. We happened to be next to the table. He fell under, while I jumped over the other side where his head lay under the table and started punching him then broke one of my knuckles in the process of hitting him in the head.

It was over. I got a lot of respect for that. I loved the attention. I felt to myself if that was all I had to do to get people to leave me the hell alone, then I would never let someone get away with disrespecting me again. It makes guys that I never even knew were in our unit start talking to me.

An inmate by the name of 210 (referring to his built in size) asked me to start working out with him 210 was cool and highly respected around the unit. One of the guys in his workout party name was G he was a Mexican I like him a lot as well we mostly did not really talk. But we had understanding; it was weird.

Big D was the funniest out of the crew. We would share silly stories. I got real cool with them, for the most part, like a brotherly love. I had learned that 210 had twenty-five years to life in prison for killing someone. He told me about it; I thought it was crazy when my boss came to my door, and they switched me to a new job. It was the library. I would become the general library clerk. I thought that it would be cool to work in the library. I would be able to read all I wanted.

There was a guy named Paul and John, who was a paralegal. Paul was the law library clerk. The ladies that ran the library was Miss Rosie and Miss Ann. The library was always pretty much quiet. My best part of the day was when the teachers used to walk by. I did not know her name, but she had a nice walk, so I always worked up front to see that walk. I enjoyed the library. It kept me from the unit and the yard for the most part of the day I only got paid twenty-five dollars a month.

I got so deep into reading. Reading was the only thing that I could use to free my mind from things that were going on in the real world.

John, being the paralegal, had access to a computer. He did not have connections to the Internet, but we did get to watch movies. The prison facility did not show R movies but did review them. And John had an inside source that used to let him watch them before they had to be back. That was how I saw a lot of movies. No other inmates had.

I had started getting depressed a lot lately, having suicidal thoughts. Since I used to see the mental health psychiatrist, I thought that I would be able to ask them for meds that would help me sleep. I just wanted to sleep the time away and not deal with the reality of what of what was going on around me from watching the commercials and listen to other people hearing how they got on medication.

I basically told the psychiatrist everything I saw from the commercials. I told them I saw dead people. I'd been hearing voices telling me to hurt others or kill myself. There was a test that I had to do. After taking them, I was refused the outpatient mental health services. They were the ones that would put me on meds, so I stood by my word that I saw dead people and they wanted me to hurt people. I was honestly depressed but overdramatized it.

The psychiatrist refused me meds but showed me how to meditate and told me that I should start writing in a daily journal. At first, I thought he was crazy. How would that help me with anything? The only thing I had going on in my favor was that I worked in the library. Most of my days was spent there, which was good because I avoided a lot of fights and whatnot that was happening around the unit.

One that I could not avoid was my bunkie. We did not really get along but, for the most part, coexisted. With the key to our room, I felt that sooner or later, he was going to let his homeboys rob me, so I tried to keep my things locked at all times.

One afternoon, I did not. I had come back from the yard to find that my watch and other small items had come up missing; they just disappeared, but I knew the play. I knew he let someone in to steal my things, and as bad as I wanted to fight, I asked him about it, he acted like he did not know what had happened. When I went to Rush, my unit counselor, and asked him for a different cell mate at first he did not want to considering this would be his fourth maybe fifth move that he had done for me in the short span I was there.

I had to tell him we did not get along I feared he had robbed me; I was told when something became available I would get the move. I left his office to go to the library another inmate told me word got around to slim I was trying to move because he and his homeboys has something to do with my things coming up missing.

As I was getting off work Smoke caught me outside asked me to come in to the day room I knew what was about to go down I put my blues on in case things got nasty I walked into the day room Smoke had six or seven homeboys While slim had his crew of homeboys ready to fight with him. To my surprise Kzoo the one that checked me about not giving him my special paper he told me I had no right putting his name in things that did not happen or was not true.

He got in my face and push me as bad as I wanted to fight Kzoo I backed down again with a broken knuckle on my strong hand it was pretty much no chance for me putting up a good fight again he had made me look soft I was not the least bit scared of Kzoo he was always catching me in the wrong place at the wrong time my homeboys appear not to be mad at me after all they all knew I had a broken knuckle.

A few days later, I was told to pack my things. I was moving to the last cell down the hall upstairs seventy-seven tops. I did not know who my new cellmate was. When I got up there and saw him, he introduced himself as T-money. I did not know T-money but had seen him around the unit time to time when I was a unit porter. I knew that T-money was the bookman for girly books, but he did not let people into his circle lightly. I got all my things unpacked and started talking to my new cellmate, getting to know him better. He told me about how he was going to the University of Michigan, going to school for engineering. A week before starting school, he and his best friends from high school were all drinking, celebrating the things to come got into a car accident where his bestfriend lost his life; T-money was serving five years in prison.

I told him a little about myself, what I was in prison for. We started talking about people that we both knew from around the unit. We had multiple mutual friends.

I found that he did not like Smoke because he had robbed him for over three hundred dollars food and property, from tapes to visiting clothes, shoes, and store goods.

I did not personally know about it, but it did not surprise me when he told me. I knew that Smoke would prey on those whom he thought was weak. Whatever the case, I would try to stay where I was at.

For a while, I was down the hall from 210 and G. There were some other homeboys that I played chess with, lock a few cells down. The only thing that I did not like was that I was right down the hall from Smoke.

T-money told me about how he worked as a tutor for a teacher at the school on the opposite days that I worked. Plus, he always had visits, which would be good because we would both at least have time to ourselves in the cells, and that was good. I was not T-money's bunkie.

Before the unit went on lockdown, Big from my workout team robbed a man and stuffed him into the locker, the unit log-in book was taken as well.

The correction officers were very upset about that. I knew it would be days before they took us down to the day rooms in two's where we were stripped searched while our rooms were shook down.

A lot of people went to the hole for knives and other dangerous contraband. The prison officers were hard on us.

The log-in book had everything in it, from everything that happened in the unit to everyone that was snitching. We stayed on lock down for four days. During those days, while being locked down for the most part, I just took the time to write.

I had to let my family know that all was well with me. My brother was locked up again, and I found a way that I could request to speak with him over the phone, prison to prison. I had not spoken with Crissy for a few. For the most part, all we did was argue or fight.

I started looking for books in the self-help and religious part of the library. I was always depressed, I needed something to change. I found a book. I still was a Muslim and went to services quite honestly, though at this point in time, I only was going to service to see Will, my sister's baby daddy.

I started reading Buddist meditation books a lot, and I liked what I started reading. Good thing about practicing meditation was my bunkie would never be in the cell, so I had all the quiet time that I needed. I decided to take the psychiatrist's advice and start to try a daily journal. I thought I would write down all the progress that I made.

One day, while in the yard, I saw someone from Bethany Creek. I thought that was cool. I had not seen him since he had gone to the hole for stabbing the other inmate outside. In the chow hall, we talked a little, caught up as fast as we could. I found out that he was living in my unit, so we decided that we could talk later.

I went and found Dre, he was playing chess. We started talking, he asked me for some advice. I liked him a lot, so I told him if I could help, I would. He told me that in the next few days, he would be going down on a ride out to Lansing to go to court.

I did not know much about Dre's case. I was told that he was in prison for selling drugs. He told me that the reason drugs were found they did a raid looking for evidence about the disappearance of his girlfriend.

I was told that he and his girlfriend at the time got into a fight and were not speaking for a few days. His girlfriend and her niece went out with another guy that knew they were enemies. Even though Dre and his girl were not talking, she got scared. The guy she was out with was showing characteristic flaws that he had never shown before.

Dre told me that he hung up the phone. Before he hung up, he heard her say whom she was with, and she was scared for life. After hanging up, she tried to call back, but he never took the call the next morning.

The police raided the hotel, found his drugs. He had been locked up ever since they raided his room. He found out that his girlfriend and her niece had been shot in the head. They were killed.

He asked if he should go to the courthouse and testify or plead the fifth. Truthfully, I had no advice to give him. I asked, Did he love her? He said yes. He told me about how he had been close to her family, and I felt bad about how everything had played itself out. My advice to Dre was to just go with his heart when it's all said and done.

Dre was going to be the one that lived with his actions. I knew just like Dre that he was going to get back out and run the streets, selling drugs. No matter how it looked at going and testifying would be considered snitching. Dre would lose all street credibility.

After showing me newspaper clippings from that day, I read how a few days later, the person that killed Dre's girlfriend was caught in a high-speed chase with the police and was arrested. He told me he was thinking about everything we talked about and would make his decision. Later that weekend, he was taken down to police department.

My bunkie, T-money, and I started talking and began to become a lot closer. T-money saw that I got really deep into meditation. He had his mom start sending me books that I wanted to read to help further my understanding, which I couldn't afford. I found that I really wanted to change my own ways of thinking. First, I wanted to quit smoking, and I did, which was hard. I was an off-and-on smoker. I felt it would just be better for my health if I just gave it all up altogether.

It did not take long before T-money and I were calling each other brothers.

Besides the little money that I had coming in working the general library, which was not much, T-money went to the store. Every time, he would put his bag on the hook in front of the door on the cell wall next to the bunks, he told me I was more than welcome to anything he had. I did feel welcome, but I was more than thankful.

T-money got offered a laundry job in the unit that would be making almost four or five times the paycheck he was making in the school, and he took the job. A lot of people who run the unit were mad about that, like Smoke. My homeboy did not like T-money. The thing I liked most about him is that as fast as they took T-money's things, he walked straight down to the ordering desk and got the catalog form, and everything they had taken, he had back in the matter of two weeks, everything and more. I thought that was funny.

I did have a good rhythm going for myself. Let's face it—no one wants to be in prison. I felt that. I was making the best of it between working out, working in the general library, and meditation. I was just doing my time. On weekends when I did not go to work, I would just play chess or sit by myself in my room.

T-money would mostly be on visits that lasted all day, which gave me a lot of time to myself. I was thankful for that in prison. Most times, inmates didn't stay cool too long.

In the course of three months, there were ten suicides, no one that I personally knew. There were people that I would see around the yard here and there, then you would just hear they had killed themselves. A few times here and there, the whole yard would get put on lockdown.

I hated that because of the suicides, the warden ordered bars to be put on the doors and windows that only lasted about a month. Just as long as it took them to put them up, they were being taken down 'cause an inmate that was hanging himself from the very bars. Someone saw it and went to tell the corrections officers. When the corrections officers got there, they could not kick the windows, because of the new bars, the inmate died, so the bars were taken back down. Killing and deaths were all too common at MTU. They got to a point there that if someone was not getting stabbed, beaten up, or dying.

Something was wrong. One day, while playing chess with Chet next to us, a white guy that was watching us play chess got blindsided with a lock in a sock he got hit so hard that he was knocked stiff. When he hit the ground, someone came over out of the crowd and started stomping him in the face. The inmate that hit him with the lock, came back to hit him in the face a few more times as if what he did at first was not enough. The man stomped him.

Me and Chet along with the rest of the yard sat and watched the whole thing, everyone started leaving what was going to be a crime scene after getting off lockdown from the incident. One of the Correction Officers said he died from his wounds. The two inmates were charged with murder.

A few days later, Dre came back from the County building after getting his things in order. He came into the day room.

He told me everything that had happened. He did testify that his girl did call and say she feared for her life. Dre told the court that she said she was with the guy that was caught in her car after the high-speed chase. The guy that Dre testified against receives two life murders. He was never going home. I asked Dre how he felt about everything.

Now that it was over, he told me that it was far from over when he got out. With the guys' homeboys that he testified against, he knew he would have to deal with that.

My homeboy Q from Bethany Creek started gambling a lot in the unit. He also was far from the Q that I knew from Bethany Creek I remember when his old bunkie use to bully him and he would not say a word, would just sit in the cell and say nothing. My cellmate Rakeeb used to speak for him. Now he had others that followed him. He was loud and wild. One time, while in the day room, he got into a fight, snatched the guy out of the chair, dragged him to the back of the day room, slammed him into the door.

Where his crew jumped him, I liked Q, but what he did had nothing to do with me. So I was kind of torn, when T-money my cellmate, told me that he started messing with him. That Q was pressuring him for money. I know where it was all going. I felt that I would not stand up for him if he would not stand up for himself, T-money started talking a lot about it.

T-money told me that if it came down to it, he would turn to punch him as hard as he could. When the next time came, I told T-money that when he did, I had his back. I would not fight against him, but felt that I had enough power to make sure they would not jump T-money.

We all knew that T-money would probably lose the fight. Unless he got a lucky punch, we were going to respect it. Everyone knew that regardless if you win or lose, it was your call if you stood your ground or stood up for yourself, that's what mattered. Not in all cases but for the most part, no one wanted to fight someone that would fight back.

Dre was telling me about a girl and how she was looking for some guys to write some of her girlfriends who also wanted pen pals. When he asked me if I was interested, at first, I did not want to. And most importantly, it was because I did not want to write a female that was locked up like me.

Dre asked me to do a favor, so I did. She wrote first, her name was Lizzy. She was twenty-three years old, up for parole next year. We started kicking things off. She was pretty cool, and besides, I needed an outlet, someone to express myself outside of prison. That was not a family member. Crissy and I still were not talking when we did all we did was say things to hurt each other. The whole ordeal with Q and T-money was starting to come to a head.

Most of the time, I was not around, so there was nothing that I could do about it. There were different situations like Q would make smart remarks to T-money, telling him to pay to be in the yard, just small things like that one night. Things turned for the worse while playing cards. Some other inmate friends with. Q walked in from a bad night at the poker table, needed someone to take it out on. They saw T-money and made him their prime target.

He came up from behind and pushed T-money's head. Told him to get everything in his cell or he was going to come and take it. I was almost sleeping, getting ready for work tomorrow, when T-money came to our cell to wake me up, telling me everything that had just happened.

I was so sick of them that I was going to end this whole ordeal once and for all. I got up and put on my clothes and walked downstairs.

Found Q with six or seven of his crew members in the TV room. I saw him, and he saw me. I called him over to see if we could talk alone. I knew that I had more power with him alone than with all his friends.

We walked upstairs to the bathroom and started talking I asked Q what was up, and why did he keep messing with T-money. Instead of me and Q talking I found myself arguing and yelling with his homeboys that had followed us.

When Q finally did start to speak he would be yelling asking what was it to me why was I protecting him saying he wanted T-money's store goods or he was going to have to lock up or get beat up.

I made a stand and took a big gamble to the good side. I took T-money's side. I told you none of that was going to happen, to get to T-money, they had to go through me. In that moment, I don't believe it was about who could win in a fight; after all, it would have been two to seven between me and Q. It was a deep respect.

When I said what I said. Everyone was quiet and looking at each other. I had given an ultimatum. I looked at him and I said, "Why you doing this? You take from him, you take from me. Besides, I know you." He knew I did. I saw that with that statement alone, I got through to him.

I asked him what I had to do to make it go away for him and for his homeboys to leave T-money alone.

They wanted five box of cigars, a month of free laundry, after taking into consideration both sides we Agreed on two boxes of cigars two weeks' worth of free wash I went back to our cell told T-money what went down.

I went to my locker to get the cigars, T-money told me no, he had it under control. He went into his locker and gave me two cigars to pay. All was well from that event. T-money and I became all the more closer.

There was an honest truth and honest friendship T-money opened up to me and started telling me about his personal life he told me about how his house got raided he had got caught with drugs in his father's home. He told me to make it all go away he had to give up the dealer to the undercover cop since I love stories I listen how one night they called him up had him go to a party to set his dealer up he went through it and got off his case I didn't look at him any differently his life was his life.

I would be a loyal friend to him eventually he would get out of prison well before I got out. If he was a true friend, I knew he would be able to do more for me on the outside, than in prison. We made a pact that as long as I made sure people stayed off his back, then he would make sure I had everything I needed. or anything for that matter money could buy.

I guess we held each other down, while my relationship with Lizzy was growing, I was writing more and more. We both started opening up to each other. During the course of being locked up, I have written here and there.

With women incarcerated mostly in the county building, I felt that it would not be any more than a prison fling once she left it was over, in truth I felt something for Lizzy but only time would tell if it was real or not.

I had received a letter out of the blue one day. It was a letter from Rakeeb, my Muslim brother from Bethany Creek. In his letter, he was telling me about how he had finally maxed out and was at home, very happy. He said he just wanted to pay his respects.

I still wrote letters with my brother that was locked up. I submitted requests to the warden to be able to call him at the prison he was at. Inmates with family members locked up we're allowed to call and talk with each other one morning my unit Arus Miss Milstar called me into her office and call my brother it was fun, talked on the phone for the first time in a long time.

For a while, I tried to keep myself positive and out of trouble by writing in my journal and meditating. Some of the guys thought I was being kind of weird, but I understood that they just did not understand why I was doing it.

I was starting to get deep into meditation. I was no longer going to Sunni service and switched to Buddhist service. The Buddhist brotherhood was very different from being Sunni Muslims. With the Buddhist brothers, we never talked. There were about ten of us going to service. G was in another religious group in the other room, so I used to see him.

Although we did not talk in service, we did do yoga together then sat in meditation for the rest of the time left. That was the best time of service for me; it was about finding your own inner peace.

Units around the prison facility were about to hold the unit elections for Block Rep. Inmates elected addressed the warden and staff about issues to make doing Time better for both inmates and staff, Two from each unit a white and black rep. A good reason for being a rep was power that came with being elected, Picking the weekly movies choosing Holiday Meals along with holiday events, that was enough incentive to run. For the most part I was not known or popular so it would be an uphill battle There was a leader from a religious group b.b that did not want me to win he started his own campaign against me adding support to my rival. As elections were held every six months inmates typically voted for an inmate with the oldest number, figuring older inmates knew the system better being that I had a 402 number the odds were against me.

B.B Was tall skinny but ripped like Bruce Lee he was doing life in prison for murder he had been in prison for 35 years from my observation I believe he was a predator he did not openly preying on people that I knew of but he was very intimidating.

The vote was held in a few days so we both started pressing for votes I felt that I had a good chance since a lot of inmates at that time where my age as the days pressed getting ready for the vote I went to the aryan boys ask for their vote, ask my homeboy G to secure the

Mexican vote, I asked most of the younger inmates for their votes as well I felt I had it locked up. When the vote came during unit count time they passed out ballots. After count time I went to wait for Miss Millstadt to post the results I had lost by thirty votes even though I was a little salty and hurt it did feel good in truth it was all fun I would do it again next time I did love to make people smile and laugh all the time. Found myself with Eastside from Detroit older inmate that was cool with the B.B I found myself mocking B.Bs walk East side cried laughing he had the most funniest Walk his arms would be kind of stiff pull to the back leg pushed back like older people he would always flood his blues if he wore them if not and wore his shorts they would be pulled all the way up to his stomach with his unique pair of gazelles glasses his hat would be rolled all the way up as if he was wearing a Jewish cap.

I started wearing my clothes like he did his walk for me just came natural when I knew he was not around I would do it around the yard everyone would laugh I just did the walk randomly here and there always making sure B.B was not around as I did not want to be disrespectful. The real funny thing was that I never told anyone who I was copying everyone just knew one day while coming back from work I walked into the unit one of the unit officers asked me to do the famous walk at first I refused. The corrections officer then called the other officer and counselor.

I knew that correction officer would not stop asking till I did it so they had me start from my cell at the end of the hall and walk towards them they wanted me to stop and turn and wave my hand like B.B did everyone who watch cried laughing that was a lot if B.B Did not know that I was going around walking like him there was no doubt he would by now even Smoke got a few laughs from the walk but after he heard about the police request me to do it he told me to stop it I was going too far, Old habits are hard to break.

A few days later while coming out of my cell after count time I walked out walking like B.B. I did not know but he was right there watching me when I see he was watching me I tried to turn around to go back to my cell, there were too many inmates behind me when I reach to where he was at he told me to keep it up he had something for me. I thought he was just talking crap. Instead of stopping, I slowed down a lot. He still managed to catch me here and there. After being caught after the fourth time, he called me into the bathroom where fights went down. I refused to go in there without knowing his intention. For the most part, I knew that he had a knife long before he showed me. As we talked, he made it very clear that he was about to see the parole board, and 'cause of the murder charge, he was only seeing the parole board every five years and did not want to do anything to jeopardize that. Most importantly, he wanted to be respected. I told him that I would stop walking like him, as I did not want to become a victim.

Dre had done his time and was about to be on his way home. We started to talk about the things that he was going to do upon his release. I tried to tell him to go to school. He told me that he was going back to the streets to sell drugs. That was all he knew—selling drugs? We had become close. I felt that we told each other things that we normally would not share with others. He told me that when he went home, he knew that no one from his family was helping him out. He said that once he got out and was on his feet, he would help hold me down. He would send in pictures, letters, and money. I believed him.

A few weeks later I walked Dre to the control center where he went home. after Dre left for the most part I started working out more with 210 and his crew. Big D pretty much laid low from when his cellmate stuffed another inmate into the locker although big D had nothing to do with the robbery as he was not even around when it happened he did get a couple of dollars that was taken so I can understand how that could play on his consciousness I did not see much of him all the while me, G, 210 and Chet played chest in our free time. I did find myself in another fight provoked by none other than Smoke I knew that it was a misunderstanding that could have been worked out things are not that easy in prison.

A homeboy from ski town said I owed him for a hair do I had him go to the store for me for what I normally charge, I guess he saw things differently. As I had already done the job after Arguing for almost ten minutes I told him that I was not going to give his money back that if he had a problem with it to come upstairs to the bathroom me, him, Chet and Smoke went into the bathroom I was not there to talk or hold the guy up as soon as we squared off I hit him in the face he was quicker than I thought he hit me back that's when I grabbed him he was a lot taller than me but I was stronger I was going to slam his head into the bathroom urinal that's when Smoke grab me for me to stop.

I was pissed but it was over I was not like that my thoughts after the fact I did not want to fight I had allowed myself to get caught up in the heat of the moment I put the other inmate in a awkward position by calling him out he would be considered soft if he did not come into the bathroom to fight my thoughts were I felt I was wrong I should not have done that I thought it was a good time to go back to the drawing board I was doing meditation and yoga really getting into it so that I could have more power and will over self to prevent things like fighting from happening I had found that I was beating myself up.

Lizzy for the most part was the only person outside of family that I talk to outside of prison after telling her what happen with the ordeal in the bathroom she did make me feel better Lizzy time was coming up for her to see the parole board we were writing a lot she started making a lot of promises like she would do the rest of the time with me send money if I needed it I believed her. I felt that we had something different then I'd ever had with anyone else I even talk to her about when I got molested as a young boy I never told or talk to anyone about that I trusted her. I believe she told me deep things about herself as well I felt that even though I still had time to do I believe we did have promise.

Crissy surprised me with a letter. I was due one from her at least once a year. I was lucky this had been two times a year. I told her about Lizzy, my feelings that I had for her. She told me that her boyfriend which was my brother's friend was on his way to the prison I was at. I act as if I was not mad, but I was very upset. I felt that as long as he did not do anything to me, then I would not do anything to him.

Things with my bunkie started heating up. One day, Smoke called me into the dayroom and was asking a lot of questions about T-money. I felt very uncomfortable, as T-money was the closest thing to family that I had. Since becoming bunkies, we had become close. We were looking out for each other, so to speak. I would not betray him. I could not turn my back on Smoke as well even though I disliked the things he stood for. With everything he did, the truth was I needed Smoke if things hit the fan or trouble was started. I needed someone to stand and fight with me. Smoke also could bring together all the homeboys, fights never happened. One on one at MTU, Smoke started asking about how much money T-money had in our cell—his shoes, clothes, hygiene products, tapes, everything because everything was money in the prison. T-money had everything. Smoke told me that he was going to rob T-money again. He said that he was going to let me know when it was going to go down so that I would be out of the way. I told Smoke that I was fine. I would not have anything to do with it. Thankfully, Smoke agreed.

I decided that I would play T-money's side to keep Smoke off him. I went to our cell and told T-money everything. The plan was to keep the door locked at all times; after all, we did have our own keys. Smoke told me everything, as far as breaking into the cell when I should not be there. I went back and told T-money.

There was a Muslim brother in the unit. Even though I stopped going to service, we still talked. He was a lot bigger than me, I felt that if anything went down he would have my back. I told him everything that was going on between me Smoke and T-money. I felt like everything that we talked about would stay between us. T-money and I locked in our cells at the end of the rock or hallway in order for Smoke to do what he wanted to do. He needed a work shift where there were correction officers that did not work a normal shift. The first time that happened was about a week after we had the initial conversation. I made it clear that I did not want anything to do with robbing T-money, so Smoke told me to leave. He was going to have other inmates knock at the door. When T-money opened the door, the inmates were going to rush in, at the same time, putting T-money down to make things appear as if it was a real robbery.

Another good thing we had in our favor, it was always a short window of opportunity.

They tried and failed. T-money laughed about it. Over a course of about a month, the same thing would happen. Smoke would tell me that he was coming. I would tell T-money to put him up on game. We would get away. Meanwhile, I was telling my Muslim Brothers everything. I could tell that Smoke was shortly going to lose his cool and was getting very desperate. Truthfully, I did not understand. Smoke was far from broke, not always. But typically, inmates that robbed other inmates were those who did not have anything. Smoke's family took care of him well. Even though I was playing a dangerous game, I can say I was having fun. After trying over and over again, Smoke did come to me one night and pulled me into the hall. He said there were six inmates three doors from my and T-money's door. They had a knife and were coming to get everything. I told him okay, to just let me get something out of the cell before they did it.

When I walked upstairs, I went into J-White's cell where Smoke had said the other inmates were. True to his word, there were about six inmates with masks or hats over their faces. I got to our cell and told T-money not to open the door no matter what. There were six guys ready to come in. T-money was not surprised that they still tried to rob him. He was surprised about six inmates down the hall. Smoke must have given them the okay because while I was in there, shorty came to the door, asking T-money if he want to buy books (girly books). Now if I would not have told T-money what was about to happen, they would have gotten him. Everyone knew T-money was a sucker for books. T-money told them no, he wasn't interested. Shorty tried to get him to open the door; T-money would not. When Shorty walked away, I left. It was our smoke break. I went outside and prayed T-money did not open that door. About ten minutes after not being able to get in, Smoke called me into the unit and said that they could not get into the cell. He told me that he wanted me to walk upstairs while unlocking my door. He wanted someone to hit me once in the head, fall out, and let them get to T-money. I tried to reason with Smoke. I told Smoke that first off, him taking from

T-money was like taking from me. I told him I did not like the idea of his robbing T-money, I was not going to play a role in it. I could tell he was very pissed, but I had to have boundaries.

That night, during lockdown in our cell, T-money and I celebrated by smoking cigars and laughing at each other. We both understood how serious shit was. I had saved T-money not 'cause I wanted to be able to hold something over his head or because he was looking out for me. It was with my meditation, trying to better understand myself and make better decisions. I come to the thorough understanding I was not a bad person. I had just made some bad decisions in my life.

The next day, before I could go to early chow, Smoke pulled me into the dayroom. I knew it was not going to be good after we sat down. Smoke was simple and straight to the point. He said that he felt like I had messed it up for him robbing T-money. He told me to give him the key to my cell or else. I sat there all confused. After everything that Smoke and I had been through, I never thought it would come to this. I could stand and fight, but I knew the odds were stacked against me. 210 walked over form another table and asked me if everything was okay. I knew that he would not let anything happen to me, but I did not want him involved in my problems. I told him everything was okay. I turned to Smoke and said that if anything in that cell was worth our friendship, then he could take it. I walked out and went to chow.

When I went back to the unit, Smoke pulled me into the TV room and told me he was sorry for what he did. He gave me back my key. He told me he had someone go into the cell but then felt bad, so he had put the few things back. He wanted me to go upstairs. T-money had come back from his call out and was in the rum offices. He wanted me to go smooth it over. I first went up to the cell to see what had been done. I saw that T-money's locker had been twisted but not broken off. Both room lockers and foot lockers they could not get into. That's why he had put everything back. He could not really get what he wanted.

I walked down to Rum's office and knocked at the door. Rumrush opened the door—I walked in. T-money was telling Rush everything. I said that I took responsibility since I was the last one out of the cell. It was possible that I had just left the door open and someone walked in. They both looked at me like I was lying. I just put my head down. Rush said I did not have to lie for Smoke and that he knew everything. Since nothing had been taken, in a week or so, he was just going to move Smoke out of the unit like it was just a random move. I did like that idea but kept it to myself. T-money and I went to our cell. I told him about how Smoke did make me give him my key; he understood. He was thankful that none of his stuff was gone. I went down to the TV room and told Smoke that I took responsibility for what happened. I lied to him. Maybe I should have told the truth; maybe I should not have. I made my bed; I was going to lie in it.

All the while, I told my Muslim brother everything that happened. I even told him about T-money telling on Smoke. I also told Ick (the Muslim brother) about how I had lied to Smoke and told him that I took responsibility for what happened.

It was about three days later when Smoke called me into the bathroom with Ick and said to Ick, "Tell Jerry what you told me." My stomach instantly hit the floor. I did not know what could have possibly happened for Smoke to have found out, but he knew. On top of that, he had told me he had me covered in the bathroom. Ick did not say anything, thank God. Smoke said that he knew everything. Smoke told me almost word for word everything that happened like I told Ick. The only thing that saved me was Ick was not talking. They closed the unit down for the gym. Smoke told me to be there; all three of us were going to get to the bottom of this.

When I got to the cell I told T-money everything. The only thing we both came up with was just to keep denying what Ick told him. We both understood that would turn out bad for the both of us. When the yard opened, I went to the gym. Smoke and Ick were sitting to the side, waiting for me. I sat down. Smoke told Ick to speak. Ick never told that he told Smoke I lied to him. Smoke took it upon himself to tell me how he found out. Smoke said that Ick told his bunkie everything that happened. Ick did not know that Smoke and Ick's bunkie worked out here and there around the weigh pit. I do not believe Ick telling his cellmate was with bad intentions considering. But I thought since it was his bunkie, it would not leave the cell. What really had me hot and bothered was that Ick, I felt, could beat Smoke or give him a run for his money. Why did he have to sell me out? Why did he not just take the fight? The fact of the matter was that Smoke had enough evidence to beat the shit out of me. If I wanted to or have someone else do it, like I said, I made my bed. I would lie in it. After about an hour with me keeping to my story and Ick keeping to his, instead of fighting me, Smoke would call me a rat (snitch). He knew that it would have the same effect as fighting me. Or that's what he had hoped for. For the most part, besides a select few, everyone hated Smoke, or a lot of people did not mess with him. So when he started spreading the story about how I was a rat, it went in one ear and out the other; no one believed him. If they did, I did not get treated like a rat. I took the heat for T-money. T-money was my brother, and I did not second-guess the decisions that I made.

After a few days, Smoke was called to the Arus office and told to move. Getting ready to go back to my unit from chow, getting ready to work, I saw Smoke. He told me I was a rat and had what was coming to me. I knew now the move was done and the only time I would see Smoke was if I went to the big yard. I let it go at that. Within the same month, Shake and Larry rode in. The first time I saw Shake was in the Chow Hall. It had been so long since the last time that I had seen Shake; he looked different. Shake was the crazy one of the crew, the one that would fight anybody, big or small, and win. When I saw him the first time, I didn't even recognize him. I was bigger than him. Shake was the brother of one of my codefendant (fat fats). Shake's case was known by everyone from home. He had jumped through a white girl's window after the football game while her boyfriend and her lay in the bed. She woke up, thinking it was her boyfriend, only to find Shake on top of her. He came to prison for rape. We did not talk about his case. We caught up on old times and talked about some of the things I missed since being gone. I was told that he was buying pills off the yard and taking them. I told him about his brother playing a part of me being in prison. He seemed like he was pissed. Whatever the case, I was just happy to be doing time with someone from back home. During the whole course of my bit, I had jailed with inmates from the county where I was from, but I knew none of them. The bad thing was that he was in a unit where I would only see him during yard.

T-money was getting ready to see the Parole Board. We all knew that he was going home. The first time, he saw the board as long as he stayed out of trouble when he saw the Parole Board. They told him that he would be going to a program called R-Sat. If he finished, he would go home. I was happy for T-money. I knew when he left, things would not be the same.

A few weeks later, Larry rode in. 210 and all my other home-boys that I messed with around the unit that shared my personal life with knew he was coming. Shake knew that we did not like each other, so every lunchtime, he kicked it with me. During all other times, he kicked it with him. The truth of the matter was that we were not beefing for the fact that he was with Crissy. But I can't say that did add to it. We hated each other from childhood like the time he slapped me like I was soft. Because he was stronger and bigger than me, I did not fight back. Or the time he and his twin brother got me drunk for me the first time and I told the police on them. There was a lot of history and reasons we did not like each other.

The first time we saw each other was coming back from the chow hall. I was with 210, Lun, G, and Big D, so I was feeling good. It was not how we planned; it just happened. Like we kind of sur-rounded him from the back, and he saw me. He must have thought I was going to do something. I will never forget the look on his face. More or less, I walked away feeling good, but I knew that one of those days, no matter how bad I wanted to avoid it, we would talk, but that was for another day.

Just like we all thought, T-money had seen the Parole Board and was told that he would be going home. I was so happy for him. I was sad inside that I would be losing my brother and best friend, the best bunkie that I ever had in prison. He had to go to a drug program. So before he went home, he had to go to a different prison; our time was short. Shake also went and saw the Parole Board and got his parole too. I was so happy for him as well. Even through the people at that time who were the closest to me were all going home, at the same time, I knew that things were going to be different, but I felt the bonds and relationships that I built with these people were long lasting and would endure. But only time would tell.

One day while going to the chow hall 210, Luna and I witnessed the longest maybe worst fight I had ever seen in prison as I had seen my share this was a lovers quarrel the fight was over an inmate I knew from around the unit and back home we even went to the same high school yet we never talked. When we walked outside going to chow, one inmate had the other on the ground and was on top of him, punching him in the face. The inmate on the bottom had his shirt over his face so he could not see anything.

The unit that I was in was the furthest from the chow hall. We walked slowly to the Chow Hall, took our time eating, and took our time getting back. They were still fighting. The guy that was winning when we left was still winning. When we got back this time, he was taunting the other while beating him up. He was punching him, saying, "Shut up! How do you like that?"

I heard the inmate on the bottom say, "Please don't hit me again. I'm sorry." No one was going to break it up either. COs were nowhere to be seen. We went into the unit. As people walked in, they were telling others that they were still fighting.

After what seemed like ten minutes after we got back from chow, an inmate that was on the med line taking crazy people's pills (that's what we called them) went to the officers' desk and screamed at the top of his lungs, "He's killing him!" If it were not for that man, I dare say he was going to kill that other man. I started talking to Shake, trying to see if he would be interested in moving over to my unit and become my bunkie when T-money rode out, which should be any day. He said yes. I liked that idea. I could not be just anybody's bunkie after having one like T-money. So I went to Miss Millstadt and told her what I wanted to do. She told me when T-money left to let her know. She would see what she could do about it.

I had seen Larry very little; we never talked. I had nothing to say to him, and he had nothing to say to me. That could have been because most of the time, I always had someone with me. One day, while I was on smoke break with guys from school, Larry came out and tried to speak with me. I did not say a word; he caught my attention when walking off. He said that I should write my son. I wanted to fight. Truth is, Crissy and I were really done talking, but I was still supposed to write my son on birthdays and holidays and send cards. I did not mean to piss Crissy off. It was selfish but the only way that I could get to her. Sometimes she tried to be kind and send pictures. I would send them back with ugly letters. So the times we did talk, we would fight.

When Larry said what he said, I knew that it would only get worse when I finally wrote. I had nothing nice to say. I told her that I never wanted to see her again and to stay out of my life. At this point, I would not have seen my son by her in almost five years. She wrote me back a few weeks later, bragging about how she had come to the same prison I was at to see Larry. I was sick to my stomach. I showed 210 my letter. He gave me the best advice I have ever received. He said after laughing he had seen how Crissy was affecting how I did the time. He told me I should just push her away for real and let it go.

Not long after that, T-money rode out. the night before he left, he gave me a lot of stuff that he would not be able to take. We did a nice big cook up and pretty much talked the rest of the night. We talked about what we were both going to do when we got out. I still had a good six years to do in prison, so he promised to help hold me down until I hit the bricks, and I believed him.

CHAPTER THIRTEEN

The Library

The next day, I walked him to the control center. We hugged and promised to keep in touch. T-money was gone. The first thing I did in my free time was I tried to get Mrs. Millstadt to move Shake over to my unit. Shake was bad on pills. When I did get to see him during chow lines, he would have me give him money to pay for them. I did not mind; that was my homeboy. I just hoped it was not going to become a bad habit once he moved to the unit.

For reasons unknown, instead of Shake moving over to become my bunkie, he packed up. They were riding him to a different prison. I was happy he was getting out of MTU; it was a hellhole. I was upset that I had to find a different bunkie. I did not have my cell long to myself when my new bunkie came to the door. He was not a ride-in from a different prison. He was from down the hall. I knew him; his name was Red. Red, for the most part, was all right. He was from the city. We never talked about our cases. Red had a broken leg from playing football on the yard. So I always messed with him with T-money gone.

I pretty much spent most of my time with 210. When I was not with 210, I played chess or was at work. I took a lot of the overtime working on the weekends. That way, when I went to my old unit, I could see Will (my sister's baby daddy).

My job was to take the book cart to everyone on Sundays. I liked that job but not when it was cold. When I was at work, I used to read. John started watching a lot of movies, mostly rated XXX. MDOC did not allow prisoners to order any kind of sexual books. You could get *Playboy*—that was about it. John started talking to me more about his little operations. I had figured someone with power had opened the maintenance closet. He and two other inmates had gone in there and stripped the DVD parts from the DVD TV combo and taken the parts to their cell and would watch DVDs in their cell. That was unheard of. If I was not seeing the DVDs for myself, I would not believe him. What was even more surprising was whom he told me was bringing the DVDs in. She was our leisure time activities director, the daughter of our prison inspector. John trusted me enough to tell me the things that he did. I would keep the things that he told me to myself. I did notice that John started getting sloppy. One day, while putting everything up, John dropped one of the DVDs fell out of his pocket right in front of Miss Roses desk. I saw it, picked it up, went to the back, and returned it to John.

He thanked me. He told me about how if he got caught doing what he was doing, he would lose his job but also would not ever be able to be a paralegal again. That was how he took care of himself. Johns family had been long gone from supporting him, so he needed the work.

Lizzy would be going home soon. We were down to our last letters. In my last one to her, I spoke about how the best thing about our friendship was how I was able to open up and be more open with her than I ever was with anyone else. Hers was one and the same line. She promised she would hold me down the rest of my way. When she got home, she told me she would write.

A while after, I started noticing how I started feeling lonely, depressed all of a sudden. I wanted out of MTU. It surely did not help when I was told that Will had packed up and rode out. Word had gotten to me late. By the time I got word, he was long gone. I was in the bathroom later when I watched my bunkie Red get jumped. He was fighting Poo; Poo was Kid's brother. Even though I and his brother Kid had gotten into that altercation when I had first gotten to MTU, we were cool.

Red and Poo had a misunderstanding, so they started fighting. Red overpowered him, which led to three other inmates jumping in and beating Red up. They did not get caught. The only thing that seemed to be hurting my bunkie Red was his ego. The fact of the matter was that an inmate by the name of Cook was one of the inmates that had jumped Red. Cook was one of the most liked inmates at MTU. He was young but respected. Everyone just like Red knew that he was going to have him lock up. Red did. I had the cell to myself for a few days; that really never happened. So I took advantage of being alone reading doing meditations and yoga.

One time 210 came to my door and saw what I was doing. After he asked a few questions, I told him that I was doing Buddhist meditation. I felt that because he did not understand, he laughed at me. I took him into the dayroom and explained to him the best way that I could. He seemed interested, so I started off by giving him some good books that had helped me out a lot. What I liked the most about Buddhist meditation was that unlike Islam or Christianity, Buddhist meditation was not a religion, so the founding beliefs did not argue against other religions. I do believe that I had, over time, come to the thought of understanding that all religions, in their own way, speak truth. Buddhist meditation helped me, showed me a way to work on myself in a way that other religions just could not at the time. If it could do good for me, I know it would be good for someone like 210. He had a long time to do in prison—might as well try to start to free himself mentally.

Now after about a month or so, I finally got my first letter from Lizzy since she had gotten out of prison. She sent me a picture with her hair down; she was beautiful. She told me how her father had gotten her a new car and how she would start going back to school. I was happy for her. She told me that she would keep in touch and stay out of trouble. As bad as I did not want to let it go or believe it, I knew that I would never hear from Lizzy again. For the most part, I spent all my time, or as much time as I could, at work. Truthfully, I was lonely and depressed. I wanted a new start. I started trying to think about ways that I could use to lock up or some way, somehow get out of that prison.

I did get a new bunkie. He was a Mexican that barely could speak English. His name was Gonzalez. For the most part, we did not talk. We could not even if we wanted to 'cause of the language barrier.

I really put my all into the work at the library. I started getting into deep conversations with John about a lot of different things. I liked him a lot. I really wanted out of that prison, so the decision that I had to make was hard, but it was the only way that I could leave MTU in a timely fashion. I would betray John's trust without snitching on anybody so that I would not get anyone into trouble. I would give up the inspector's daughter for bringing in the CDs. In return, I would ask for a close-to-home transfer.

A few days later, while on smoke break, I saw the ADW of Housing Unit going to her office. ADW is short for Assistant deputy warden. As bad as I wanted to speak with this lady, I could not do it and let other people see me. If any other inmate saw me talking to the lady alone, I would be labeled a rat. I needed to avoid that kind of attention. I was lucky enough that at the time, the ADW came through there was no one around. I approached her and told her that I might have some information that she might want to know about. But I would talk to her about it alone. She told me to come with her to her office. When we got there, she told me to have a seat and to tell her what was on my mind. I told her about how I knew a head figure from the administration, bringing things in that was not allowed. She told me to go on. I told her I was not interested in having this conversation without her giving me a favor in return. She told me to go on. I told her I wanted to request a close-to-home transfer in the help that I provide.

All the while, in the office, there was a big window that faced the smoke break. I could be seen out there. Every time I thought inmates were looking in that direction, I would squat down in the chair so that no one would see me. The fact of the matter was no matter how it was looked at, I was snitching. I justified it because I was telling on someone in the administration instead of one of the inmates. She called the inspector into the office. I knew that the lady that was bringing in the contraband was the inspector's daughter. I wanted to approach this differently. As much as I wanted to back off, I had said too much. I had to proceed when the inspector came into the office and agreed to the terms. If anything that I told them turned out to be true, I would get a close-to-home transfer. I did not want John to get into any trouble. I also did not feel it was appropriate bringing the inspector's daughter into the plots scheme. I told the administration that I could get them rated XXX DVDs that were being brought to the facility. The ADW wanted to know where the DVDs were and who was bringing them in. I asked for a little time—I needed some time to think and put it together so that John and his other inmate friends would not get into trouble. I told the ADW and the inspector for my safety, I did not want to be seen speaking to them in the open. I trusted the councilor in my unit. Ms. Millstadt—we would communicate through her. It was agreed. I walked back to work set and just thought, How could I put this together without getting any inmates in trouble? I knew by John's word that the leisure time activity director, the inspector's daughter, was bringing in the contraband. John also told me that for the safety of getting caught with the DVDs, he kept the DVDs in the hobby craft room. I would want to speak with Miss Millstadt to see what she thought.

A few days later, Ms. Millstadt called me into her office. She told me she had talked with the ADW. I kept nothing from the counselor. I held out on the part about knowing were the DVDs were. When I told her what I thought about the inspector's daughter being the one bringing the DVDs in, she told me that I was smart for not bringing that up when I was in the ADW office. The counselor and the ADW wanted me to watch for when John got on the computer. They wanted me to tell the ADW when John was on the computer with the DVDs. They wanted me to catch him redhanded.

I agreed to Mrs. Millstadt's face, but inside my head, I was not going to do that. As much as I wanted to leave that prison, I did not want to do so at the expense of John, but that's what it looked like it was coming to. I went back to the cell; I had a lot to think about.

After thinking for the most part of the night, I said to myself that I would play their game. I would give him up. Every day for the next month, I tried to catch John watching the DVDs. The times that I thought he did, I would ask for a bathroom break and run to the unit to tell Mrs. Millstadt to send the troops. Every time, it worked in John's favor 'cause almost every time, something happened that would not let the process work. John would be off the computer. If he was, it would turn out to be a game of solitaire. I was running to the ADWs office so much that other inmates started looking at me funny or would start making little jokes, calling me Rat or green tag which meant the police, but if they only know I had a program. I would act like I had important paperwork, which really was a front to get into the office. So the other inmates would not think anything was up.

So much time went on with so many results, but I know the administration believed me to be lying, trying to just ride out. That was till shit hit the fan in John's unit. John's other inmate friends kept the DVD player that was stolen from the school maintenance locker in their typewriter. John's friend was raping his bunkie. While watching the DVDs, the bunkie walked to the officer's desk and told the COs that he was being raped. For proof, he spit semen in a bag. John's homeboy was not even a week into his marriage and was going home in ten days. He was taken to the hole, where he would await the state police to come get him to charge him with rape. The inspector believed me then. Everyone that worked in the library went to the hole. I did not and was very upset about it. I did not want to be looked at as different. Why did I not go to the hole? I did not want that kind of attention. I also realized that it was now or never. If I did not give the DVDs up, they would find them themselves, then I would not get awarded the ride out. It was either find where they were or not ride out, all that I had been doing would have been for nothing. It did not take long for me to come up with what I was going to do.

The next day, I went to work all by myself. Ms. Rose and Ms. Ruth knew what I was doing. I got dirty looks from them. They never said anything, but I knew they knew. My ARW, Mrs. Millstadt, did not come in as early as I went to work. On the first smoke break, I went back to the unit and got into her office. I told her about everyone that worked in the library went to the hole. She told me that she knew about what went down with the DVD player in John's unit. I told her to call the inspector. I knew where the rest of the DVDs were. She did, and I went back to work. While sitting in the lobby with Ms. Fox for about an hour after the fact, I saw ARW the inspector walk by the window. I saw her hand in about twenty CDs and DVDs. She looked at me and smiled; it was done.

Later that day, while going to a bathroom break, I passed the inspector in the hall. That was not uncommon with her and the ADW's office being in the school. Walking past me, she told me that I was riding out. When I got back to work, I overheard Mrs. Rose telling Ms. Ruth that John was going on an emergency ride out (transfer) to a different prison facility. He would never be allowed to work as a paralegal again. That bothered me more than I thought it would. Truth is that I liked John. I really did. When I struggled, he helped. When I was depressed, he made me laugh. The only thing that I could possibly think to try to make myself feel better about what I did was say and accept to myself that I made a conscience decision—one that I would have to live with the rest of my life.

Chet, Lun, 210, and Big D, everyone that I called friends or worked out with, I started telling them that a family member was sick and I was being awarded a close-to-home ride out. I explained that is why I was in the ARW's office so much. For every question they asked, I had an answer. Two times after that back and forth from Mrs. Millstadt's office to the library, I was allowed to really call and speak with my brother at a different prison. When other inmates saw that, I told them that I was talking to a member of the family that was on their deathbed. Everyone believed me, so I wanted to ride out.

It was close to Christmas time for the most part. Every time I talked to the ARW, I was asking when was I going. I stayed on her back. She told me to be cool; my time would come. Those days before Christmas, the last day that the MDOC did transfer before the holidays, I was told to pack my things. I was riding out. I got all my things together, packed my personal property, took it to the property room, and kicked it with all my friends. Before I left, I don't know why, but I wanted to tell someone what I had done. I wanted someone to know the truth. 210 was one of the only inmates there at MTU that I would remain friends with outside prison. After going to dinner, I asked him to come into the dayroom. I left nothing out and told him everything after it was all out. He told me that it was something that he would not have done; nonetheless, it is what is is—you move on without making habits of that.

CHAPTER FOURTEEN

SPR

Later that night, the administration gave us a holiday day event of Karaoke. 210, Lun, and I went through all the negative BS from being in prison. I can honestly say that we had a good time. The next morning, I walked to the control center. I saw Mrs. Millstadt. She said, "I told you you would ride out," and I did. After about an hour, I was on the bus heading for what I thought was a close-to-home ride out. Every time I asked the COs where I was going, I was told SPR Pine River in the total opposite direction of where I was promised I would be going. I had been lied to. I am not going to try to express how used and dumb I felt at that moment. I accepted it for what it was and would move on when I arrived at SPR. I really did not know how to feel. For now I be sleeping in the open seven man cubes during my time in prison. I had heard about stories of there kind of living conditions, and not good stories, I might add. I was also not used to being able to come and go as I please. The prison yard was open pretty much all day besides chow lines and prisoners' count time. Other than that, it was come and go as you please. Another plus that I liked was there would be no inmates with life around. All prisoners here were close to going home. Truthfully, I did not understand why I was there. Because of so-called good behavior, I had been moved down to level one. Most people here were going home within two years, maybe four years at most. I was going into SPR with the MTU mind frame. If anybody gave me problems, shut them down, fight, gain some respect for myself.

After getting my property and going to my unit and bunk, I was getting introduced to my new bunk mates. There was my bunkie C-X, who by the way had already seen the Board and would be going home soon. Across from us was a young city boy named Neno. He did not have a bunkie at the time. Behind the wall of lockers were Curt and Richard. Across from them in the one bunk was Old School. Kurt was by far the nicest to me. When I was unloading my things, he saw I did not have much. So he went to the locker and got me some extra things. I was thankful for that. But I knew that I would watch him. I was not use to other inmates just being nice to be nice. So when other inmates like Kurt did what he was doing, it would bring me back to the days of Bethany Creek when I was around all those predator inmates.

SPR was nothing like MTU with in my first hour of being around the unit and my new cubbies, I knew that all the fighting and stabbing days were over. I still would keep my guard up; it was just habit to. I went to the yard to see if anybody there was from where I was from, any homeboys. To my luck, I found out that Will was there (the father of my sister's kids). I knew he alone would make my transition a whole lot better. Even though we were in different units, I would be able to talk to Will all day if I wanted to, unlike in MTU. Even though I did not know anybody, he took me around and introduced me to all the homeboys. A few of them knew my family members—that was all right. Chad was there. Chad was from my hometown. From the other side, we were on the same football team. I personally knew him and his brothers and sister. Newell was there as well; he was in the unit next to me. Newell had been at MTU. I remember him, but he left before I really got to know him. So after meeting all the other homeboys, later that night, I decided to just get on a regular plan of working out and going to service. My bunkie CX told me that I could work out with him and his partner, which was a guy named QX. Will worked out, and I could have joined his crew, but my bunkie seemed okay, so I said yes. So that's what I did.

I put in a call out for Buddhist meditation services and worked out. For the most part, I kept quiet, staying to myself to get to know how the prison was run. When I was not doing any of that, I would hang out with Will, Newell, and Chad. We were all jokesters, so it was always fun and games when I was with them. Will, in his free time, would hang out with other inmates, inmates that me and the other homeboys would question his association with.

For the most part, we kept it to ourselves. I noticed how all of them were taking pills—sleeping pills mostly. When I was at home, I liked downers—they were cheap—so when I was not working out free time, I would take sleeping pills and would mostly sleep weekends away. Only Will knew; I kept that to myself.

I started to get to know others around the unit. I was also getting to know the unit COs in first, second, and third shift; all seemed okay. First shift had a lady named Ms. P. Everyone warned me about her, but she was harmless; I liked her. Second shift had Hadler and Ms. B. They both were all right. From doing time, I had learned that officers only wrote tickets and were assholes if the inmate stayed in trouble and was an asshole.

One day, right in yard, I was introduced to a new homeboy that had just rode in; his name was Damon. After talking to him about other inmates or the people we both knew from home or the MDOC, I learned that his father was shorty from MTU, the inmate that I used to talk to when I went to the hole, trying to lock up. I thought that it was a small world. I told him about his father helping me to come out the hole and face my problems. He said that it sounded like his father. Damon was young when his father had gotten locked up. He told me what he remembered mostly was that he was silly as hell. Even though he loved his father he told me about how right now, they just were not on speaking terms.

I thought that Pine River was not bad, comparing it to MTU. SPR had good food. There were hardly any fights, no stabbing whatsoever. Everyone for the most part had that going-home attitude or swagger about them on like all the other joints I had been to. I stayed on the same program for the first few months. CX (my bunkie) finally walked to the Control Center and went home. I would have to work out with Will or find a new workout partner. I requested to get the bottom bunk before my new bunkie came.

My new bunkie's name was Mickey. Mickey seemed all right. He was a stock broker, in prison for selling dope to an undercover cop. We talked a little. I showed him around the unit. He said that he wanted to work out so we could become partners. I had my eyes on becoming the unit rep. I still knew how it felt to take a loss. The block rep, Gibbs, was on his second term and had to step down. I also understood by now being the block rep for the warden was a popularity contest. A good thing that I had going for me was that a lot of inmates were short term, so they would come and go. Even though I had been down for a while, I was not considered a fish any more by my number that was still young. Gibbs was a Mobit, and I could not stand them. Something about him was very different. He was a lot older, took no shit, and was a fighter. I had seen him run up on and pin another inmate. We started talking a lot. He told me that he would help me get elected block rep. So I signed up. I went up against like five other inmates. I won big. I had most of the votes thanks to Gibbs. With power comes responsibility, and I took them head on. Being on the warden's form was no biggie. I would get my job that I had to do and go to the monthly meetings to be the voice of the population to the administration. For that, at the end of the six-month term, I would get a Leadership Certificate. When I went to the first meeting of inmates to get voted my position, I learned that was yet another popularity contest. Since I was not known, I really did not get the job I wanted, but I did get a good one. I was voted food rep. In short, my job was to get to all meals before anyone else did to test if they were good or not. I would grade all meals. I also was in charge of picking all the holiday menu; that was cool. I found fast that being the food rep had a lot of advantages; they tried to spoil us. The first day on the job, the white rep and I were told that if we took care of them, they would take care of us. If we did not report them to the warden, they would feed us well. I saw that also when I went to breakfast at around 5:30 a.m, the first shift _____ would be coming in. All other inmates would be sleep; only a few workers would be around.

I started talking with Ms. P a lot. I did not take it as anything but good conversation. I had been growing my hair since I had been in prison. I thought that it was time for something different. So I cut it all off. It was around that time that I started sleeping more and more. I still worked out with Mickey. I found out even if I wanted to slack off, he would not let me. We would almost go into a fight. The fact that he stood up for me meant a lot to me for some reason. I mean, I'm nobody when it comes to threats, but there was something about that altercation wherein we both found more respect for each other. I had a yard crew job that paid next to nothing forty hours a week. I would only get twenty a month if I was lucky. Mike started looking out for me; he would buy enough food to take care of us both. All he asked in return was that I worked out, and since I did that anyway, everything worked out good.

Not long after, I received my first letter from T-money, my old bunkie. He was having a hard time getting through the class. Everything besides that was going well, that he would be home by the next time that I heard from him. I had also gotten cards from his mom in the past. She would send one along with John's card. In her card was a $75 money order to get me a foot locker. That was one of the big things that happened to me in prison. What I enjoyed most was he did it when he did not have to. I did not place any monetary value on our friendship. I just thought that was the coolest thing ever.

One day while on the yard, the new rides came. I thought that I saw G from MTU. I was so far back from the crowd I really could not tell. Later that night, when the yard was closed G, came into the unit. It was him. I was happy to see someone that I liked and got along with. But I knew that G would be a part of my circle. Another good thing was that we were in the unit together. I let him go and get himself unpacked. When I was not working out with Mike, I was still taking a lot of sleeping pills. During that time I would take them, the only thing I would do was eat. I still kept what I was doing to myself; only Will knew about the pills.

Speaking of Will, I did spend a lot of time with him. We looked out for each other and had each other's back if anything went down. One of the homeboys that was from where me and Will were from went home. I can say while he was there, he kept Will on point. When he left, Will went wild. Everything that everyone did not want to talk about with the funny people Will would be around came to a head. Will was openly being with the homosexual and did not care what others said or thought about it. The other homeboys were pretty much on him about it. I stood back and would not judge him if that's what he wanted to be into. That would be on him, as long as he did not bring it around me—that's how I felt. I also had a past, one that I did not want people to know about from Bethany Creek. I felt that I would just play the side and let him figure things out for himself.

The next time, I talked to my sister, the one he had kids by. I had to tell her about him; it was only right. I talked to my sister about a month later. I told her about Will. It surely did not surprise me when she told me that she already heard about it. People talk and gossip, that's just how it is. I told her how I was sorry to have to confirm it. Will was out of control. I had another homeboy that took a bunk in my cubb. He moved to my unit from a different unit for fighting. I personally did not know him. But others from home that did know him told me to watch out for him. He did not have a TV, so time to time, I would let him watch my TV. If he did not have any money, I would do his hair for him. He seemed all right. I just took to calling him Wonn or Ski town.

Everything was going good for me as block rep. I was eating probably the best I had ever eaten my whole life. Working out with Mike as much as I did had me looking really good. My block rep term was coming to an end. I would have to run again but without the help of Gibb's. He had been sent next door to the other prison. I was well-liked, so I was not worried. I ran again and won big. I was enjoying being the block rep. I had a little power. The rep picked menu changes, picked holiday meals, and special events. Like things that would be on _____ the prisoner stores. There was certainly some good and bad about being the unit rep. We started having once-a-month meetings with my unit counselor. Ms. Flight, she was fine as hell but very mean. The only part I liked about those meetings that I would be able to talk to Mrs. P. I would show Mrs.

P my pictures from home. She did not share her personal life with me, because it was not allowed. Besides that, she did not have to. Everyone knew she stayed at the bar and was on her second divorce, two different men that worked at the prison facility. One was a CO; the other, a maintenance man. Everyone thought she was a wreck. I would make her laugh most the time. And whenever time permitted, I would share small conversations with her.

Kurt and Richard started telling me about things coming up missing around the cube. We had the same cubbies besides Wonn and Neno's bunkie, Heavy. Heavy pretty much stayed to himself, and he was on our side of the cubb. It was quickly narrowed down to Wonn. It had nothing to do with me. I did not like him stealing if it was him. I also did not like everyone coming to me about it, like I had power over him to stop it. It must have had something to do with us being homeboys, I guess. A thief is a thief, and if it was him that was doing it, I knew that it would not be long before I felt the sting.

Shortly after a while, I did. One night, Wonn asked me to braid his hair. I did; he paid me in some batteries. I had no use for them, but money was money, and I did not refuse. I went to bed. I left the batteries on my table. I did not think nothing of it because like I said, as long as I had been in that cubb, I could leave things out and did not have to worry about my things coming up missing. When I got up the next day, the batteries were gone. I kept my cool. I figured something had happened and I would find out. I started asking around. Or better yet, people would see the look on my face and ask me what was wrong. The finger all the way pointed to Wonn. I was not going to call him out on it if I did not have the facts. Everyone on my side of the cubb ended up in there—me, Mike, Nemo, and Heavy. Wonn walked into our conversation and started yelling that nobody was going to do this or that to him. Saying he would give it to anyone had something to say about him behind his back. I guess word got back to him that everyone assumed that he took what was missing. Truthfully, I was very pissed that he would take from me. After all the nice things I did for him that I did not have to. I was willing to sweep that under the rug, when he started yelling and the other inmates started looking up and down the Rock (hallway) and looking over the wall. I reluctantly put on my shoes under the table. I knew that we were going to fight. After getting my shoes on while he went on with his little rant, I walked to the cubbs entryway to make sure there was no one around. But we did have a nice crowd by now. Inmates were walking by, looking up and down the hallway, even over the wall. I went in and hit him with a three-piece combo that sent him reeling back. He grabbed at me. Wonn was bigger than me. I was stronger, and it made all the difference. After a few more good hits, the fight was broken up. Justice had been done. Truthfully, I did not care about the batteries. It was about respect, and I had just earned some.

After the fight, I went into the dayroom and spoke with G about all the events that had taken place. G had my back, and I was thankful for that. While in the dayroom talking with G, Neno walked in and gave me the batteries that he had taken; that was not surprising to me. I went to the yard to tell all the other homeboys so that there was no misunderstanding. I did not want Wonn to go starting anything new. During the fight, I had messed up my ankle somehow. I could walk on it. It was very painful, without the duties of going to work out.

For the next two weeks or so, I started taking pills every day. I also would start to notice that Ms. P was acting differently. She was showing me attention, or that could be what I took it for. It was small things like when other inmates would throw water on me in the shower. She would look in the shower room and laugh at me. Or when I would brush my teeth while taking a piss, she would have something to say about it. I never quite caught onto anything out of place.

One morning, while everyone was sleeping, when I had to go test the food, when I got back to the unit, she called me to one of the only blind spots in the unit. Everyone was sleeping, and no one was around. She asked me to carry something for her. When we were alone, she paused as if she was looking for me to say something, but I had no clue.

After a while I got a surprise letter from Crissy. It had been a while since I had heard from her or anybody for that matter from home, besides my brother that was locked up. As hard as it was, I was just trying to be over Crissy. I could not do time with her being a part of my life. I told her to just stay out of my life for what she did when I was at MTU. Coming to visit a man when I had not seen our child in over five years, was the final straw. I put the letter in my locker and refused to even read it, yet I could not just destroy it or throw it away. I should have. After stressing for about a week thinking about the letter the whole time, I opened it. She was trying to make amends by telling me how sorry she was. Her and Larry had broken it off. My son had been asking about me. She wanted to bring him to see me. We had been playing with each other's hearts so long That I was just done with it, so I refused to even respond. She kept writing. I was getting letters every other week and trying not to read them, only to read them and not be able to eat or sleep. She was trying to get back in. I felt all the while, my mind was playing tricks on me. The mind told me to let it go. She was not right, but the heart would not let go. Eventually, I gave in and responded. She told me about how she needed to talk to me face-to-face and that she wanted me to see our child. I agreed and did the paperwork for her and my son to get approval to come visit me. Nothing happens overnight through the MDOC, so it would be a few weeks before she could come see me.

By the time all the paperwork was done and approved, we set a time and date. She did not come. I was very mad. She told me that something did come up that did not allow her to come, so we made a different date.

A homeboy named Batman had been at SPR for a few months. For the most part, I would just say hi or bye. We did not talk; really I thought he was crazy. The same day, for the second date, Crissy was supposed to come see me. Before visiting hours, I was talking to another homeboy from home. He started telling me about how he had seen pictures of Crissy in Batman's photo book. I had to get ready for the visit. The whole time, my brain was trying to understand. How could Batman have pictures of Crissy? The only reason I could come up with was through Larry. Larry must have given him one. I should have been getting ready for the visit. I walked outside to give Batman a door call to politely ask if could see his pictures. I figured the worst case, I could prove that she was the mother of our child. Since we both knew that he did not even know her and that the pictures were given to him by another, he would not let me cash him out for the pictures. He was at work, so I went in the unit and waited for Crissy to come. I ironed my clothes and kicked it with G and Mike. I was happy that I not only was going to see Crissy but also my son the first time in a long time.

She was supposed to be at the prison at around 2:30 p.m. So when 3:00 p.m. came around, I started to worry. She did not have a cell phone, so I could not call and confirm that she was on her way or not. At around 5:00 p.m., I knew that she was not coming. I was mad and getting myself upset again. I had brought this upon myself and I should have just not let her in.

Later that night, I saw Batman come out of work and I asked him if I could see his photo book. "Later," he told me; the yard was going to close. The next day, I caught Batman going to the backyard to work out in the weight pit. I stopped and asked him about the pictures. Someone must have told him that I knew about them because he got defensive, trying to fight. I did not want to fight Batman. For one, I had nothing coming. Batman stood 6 feet tall or better and weighed easy 230 pounds, no fat. One of the other homeboys pushed him back and told him that's not what I was there for. I took the chance to walk away from the situation while I could. I was very mad and needed someone to take it out on. The only person I could think of was Crissy. I started beating myself up. For one, I knew that she would do this to me. Somebody told me to let her back in. I did and got hurt. I made up my mind to just push her away and just be done with it. The other times we fought were just bickering back and forth. I just like her knew what we could say to each other and get away with it. But now, I would go past all that. I would say the things I needed to say to push her away for good. Truthfully, it was a hard decision to make, one that needed to be made. Or I was just going to make it. She had the power to completely throw me off my square.

I went in that night to write all the things I needed to say to get rid of this woman, out of my life for good. I sealed it and sent it out. Even though it hurt and it did hurt really bad, I felt that it was just best for me both of us in the long run. About two weeks later, I got a response. She kept it short and simple. She told me that she was leaving and that I would not need the address 'cause she would never write me again as long as I was in prison. She told me how my words did not hurt her feelings and that she would raise our child alone. She ended the letter with a big "Fuck you!" at the end. I knew Crissy. I knew as long as I was in prison, I would never hear from her again. As best I could, I let it go and moved on. It was hard but I did.

I started to become all right with the second-shift unit COs, Hadler and Mrs. B. Sometimes they did, but officers were not allowed to watch the dayroom TVs. I started letting Hadler watch mine and in return, I would get stuff from the outside that I was not allowed to have or could get from the inside. I thought it was an even trade. It was mostly food, but there were other things like books. If other inmates got shaken down and had things they were not supposed to have like, say, girly books, I would get heads up that they were in the trash and I could go get them. They would also look up other inmates, what they were in prison for, or look up fine women in MDOC so that I could write them. Looking up inmates around the whole unit was one thing in itself. I could not believe how many inmates were there that had sex cases. We looked up almost the whole unit and honestly found that over half the unit had sex cases, most of them kids. That was also around the time that Hadler showed me SPR was made to mostly hold inmates with sex cases.

I had started getting a lot of questions from other inmates to why I spent so much time in office or around the COs. But I always used being on the warden's form as an excuse; it always worked.

Hanging out with G, we started getting really close. He even asked me to be his best man at his wedding. I thought that was cool. He also told me about the reason he was in prison. He said that he and one of his friends from home were at his friend's house when some guys came knocking at his door. Beefing with other gangs were common. A Rival gang, before kicking in the door, shot the house up. In the process, shots fired killed G's homeboy. G said the only thing that saved his life was that before they came into the house. He wiped blood from his friend's body on him. The gang came in and saw them both bloody and left.

Sometime later, G was at a party when a gang member from that night that G's friend was gunned down showed up at the party were G was at. One thing led to another, G and one of his homeboys shot and killed that guy at the party. They rolled him up in a rug and threw him in the river. He was eventually caught and charged. That was the short version. Secretly, I went later to Hadler to look on the computer to see if G was telling the truth. For the most part, he had done what he said he did. Him telling me what he did made our bond stronger.

Everything in my cube was fine me and Wonn never really got that cool after him stealing as he eventually left are cube things with Kurt and Richard was a little weird knowing they both had sex crimes against twelve-year-old little boys and girls. I did try not to pass judgment. It's kinda hard when put in perspective as if it was one of your kids they touched. I found that when we were alone, Kurt was freaky. I would sell him simple books. That would be for two or three dollars for like five or ten; he was out of control. Neno, Mike, Hadler, started playing board games risk was our game of choice. We would get lost playing that game for days.

One night, things took a turn for the bad. As inmates, we were not allowed to have spinners or dice so that we could not gamble, so we used cards. How we used them, it was very possible to cheat. I did think Neno was cheating instead of getting into it. I said that I quit and walked out. Neno walked out behind me, pulling his blues up, which told me that he was getting ready for confrontation. I stopped to see what he was about. He walked right in my face. Before he could say anything, I told him to come back to our cubb; we should have taken care of this a long time ago. He came back with me. We stopped in front of the cubb's entryway. I told him to go in. He would not. I looked up the hall. Ms. B was right there. I did not care about them; I was off my square. Nemo was probably just as fast as me, if not faster. Sizing him up, I felt that his endurance was, more than likely, better than mine, but I knew that I was stronger. Even with Ms. B watching or in sight of us, I punched Nemo in the face, went for his legs, and slammed him. I landed on top of him. He tried pulling me down to his face to bite me. I bear-crawled to bring him into our cubb.

By that time, I was overpowering him to begin punching him in the face. That's when Mickey yelled, "Stop, Jerry, Ms. B is coming." I knew that she had seen me. I told Mike it was too late; she had already seen me.

Mickey yelled, "Get off of him and pulled me off Neno!" I jumped on my bed Neno jumped on his, Ms B was at our door way. Since I always played around the unit with others. I'm assuming that she gave us the benefit of the doubt and thought that we were playing. She asked is everything all right? All three of us said yes she walked away. She walked up the hallway I walked out the unit to grab some air to cool off. I did not know that Neno was getting his home-boys together to come jump me. Neno was a member of the MO's. From far-off, I could see Neno and three other inmates behind me. I kept walking in hopes that I would run into someone that would fight with me if need be.

As I got to the backyard there was G. I got to him as quickly as I could. I gave him the story of what just had happened. I told him how there were four of them behind me. He told me that he and Polo had my back and not to worry. As I walked away, G and Polo went to confront Neno and whom he had with him. I watched just in case they started fighting. I would have to go back and help. That was not the case; he had them going back to the unit. Whatever he had said cooled them off. As I started walking back to the unit, trying to gather my thoughts, I started seeing other inmates that I knew had my back starting to come to the yard. Even though you think some-one will fight with you, it does not necessarily mean that they will. I felt good seeing the support that I had. By the time I had reached the unit, a mutual friend of Neno and me approached me and looked like he wanted to fight. I tried to explain best as I could that things had happened so fast, and I did not want it to go that way, but it had.

I found Neno. We talked and got somewhat of an understanding and agreed that it was done. I did not 100 percent trust that it was over. Neno had a black eye. I feared that he would try to catch me in my sleep. I had seen it done too many times—while one inmate thinks that a fight or beef is over, the other is secretly planning with a lock in a sock or to thoroughly pour boiling water on them. I found G talked with him; he told me not to let my guard down. I thanked Polo. Even though I did not know him, he was going to help me fight. Later after the yard closed, after everything settled down, I notice a nice long scratch. That would turn into a scar later on my arm. I went to Ms. B for a Band-aid. I gave her a funny look. She gave me the Band-aid and I went to my cell. She had seen and knew what had happened. What was not said was understood. As long as Neno did not tell on me, I would be okay.

Later that night, I set up chairs around my space so that if anyone came next to me, I would be able to hear them coming. I also slept with a phone book on top of my face so if I did not hear the chair, the book would stop the force of the lock or water from burning my face. I slept like that for about a week or so just in case I would get tricked.

Later, Neno was told to pack his things; he was riding out. I was happy that they moved him. I was getting tired of sleeping like that. Even though it was not told to me, I knew that he was moved cause of the fight. I wanted to leave as well. I would think and come up with a plan to leave that prison

Neno's replacement name was Mickey white guy 6'2'" cool as hell. Now in the cubb we had Mickey my Bunky and Mickey the new guy. So we did not get names confused we called the new guy slim meanwhile as Neno was gone me and my Bunky bond became stronger he was pretty much feeding me looking out for anything I needed.

I did have the yard crew job, but I was ready to quit. I had saved enough to get a new color TV. I talked with Hadler and Ms. B to speak with my boss on the yard crew to get me as a unit porter. I went through hell to go through this process, but after doing 30 days locked in my cube the day I got moved. Mickey my bunkie suggested that since I had been on the wardens form and new most of the inmates around the unit that I should start a store. Store inmates got robbed. The money was good, but there was a lot that came with it. A store is where I would go to the prison commisary store. I order one hundred dollars in food. As other inmates needed the store items that I had, I would give it to them and charge them interest with it. Basically one hundred would turn into one hundred and fifty, so on and so forth. I still had a lot of time to do at that point, and Mike was not going to be there to feed me forever. Besides, he was offering the startup money if I agreed to only deal with a few inmates to keep things down.

After a while, I found that between bunkie Mikes in my cubb and Kurt and Richard, my cubb was selling me out. It felt good taking care of myself and not having to worry about Mike cooking up something or how much I would make from work to feed myself and attend to my hygiene. Slim started getting out there and sometimes couldn't make store, so he started giving me his pills. He was getting seroquel and oxycontin as if I needed them. I was already buying sleeping pills off the yard. Oxycontin alone could bring in a pretty penny, inmates spend anywhere from $20-$60 easy. Slim even had his mom writing me sending me money directly. He was not only buying me clothes but shoes, socks, watches, earrings—anything that I wanted. The crazy thing was all I had to do was be his friend and listen to him. Everything with Will, Chad, and Newell started coming to a head. As best as I could I tried to avoid what I knew was to come with that whole situation. For the most part, every time Will was not around, all the homeboys that hung around us or were from where we were from back home would talk about him behind his back. When they did when I was around, I would walk away and try not to be involved. After a while, it just became common that inmates talked about him for openly being with the homosexuals. G saw Will on the yard hugged up with his head on the other homosexual inmate's lap. When he came into the unit and told me, I knew that I had to say something to Will. It was just getting out of control. Truthfully, I was not judging Will. I just could not believe that he was being so open with what he was doing. I should have come at him a better way. But I tried to have him choose. I took Chad, Newell and asked Will to either be with us or be with them. Everything took a turn for the worse after that. Will went back to his unit and sent out one of his homosexual friends to fight me. That was the only way that I could take it. I didn't know much about the inmate, just that when Will was with all his homosexual friends, he was around. I'm sure the only reason we did not fight was he would have to fight Chad and Newell as well. That did not keep him from speaking his mind. We had a heated conversation about Will and the company that he was keeping. I found out then that Will had been talking about me a lot as well. The inmate said out loud, "Jerry you should have nothing to say after what you did at Bethany Creek!" That was like a slap in the face. I paused and denied what he was talking about and ended the conversation. How did Will know what happened at Bethany Creek? And why would he share it with someone else? I needed to talk to him. As much as I wanted to avoid the conversation, well truthfully, it was past due.

At dinner, I gave Will a door call. He came out to speak with me, and I put everything on the floor. He openly admitted that he liked boys and that's what he was going to do. I told him that I never had a problem with that. I just wanted him to know the things he did affected both of us. If something happened, I would be there to support him. I felt that it was wrong of him to leave me out thee loop even if he was messing with boys. Will tried to talk to me as if I liked Boys, but I had nothing to say about that. I didn't even ask him about what he thought he knew about Bethany Creek. I just denied it all. While walking to my unit after dropping Will off at his, I knew that our friendship would be forever changed. Thinking back on the events that day although things turned out OK things could have gotten very bad when his homosexual friend came to check me. Besides that, he was going to openly be with homosexuals I did not want to be a part of that I had my own secrets I did not want to add to them I would now distance myself from will.

I still was looking for ways to leave that prison. I really don't know why—everything was going well. For me, I was really eating good. For the most part, there were good people around me. I had a good cubb; the store was doing good. I had a good relationship with all the unit Cos. For the most part, I had it made. The problem was I had made up my mind to leave, and there was no turning back from that.

A few days later, East Side rode in, or that's the name I remember him by when we talked, because they moved him into my unit. He made it known, in a cool way. I would say that he remembered me from Bethany Creek and everything that happened to me. I could not believe it. I felt Bethany Creek was haunting me. The things that happened to me there would follow me for the rest of my life. I understood it for what it was; he had something to hold over my head. To have power over me, with him knowing that about me, the thing from Bethany Creek, he had me in the palm of his hand. The only thing I could do was wait to see how he used it.

The next day, I was doing a lot of thinking, having a lot on my mind, I needed an outlet from prison. I could not or did not really want to talk to anyone. I would not be seeing Mrs. P; she was on her vacation. I had a lot going on upstairs. I walked in to the chow hall to test the food. I would say I was not being aware of my surrounding. I led myself right into a trap; the COs that I did not know that night as I did proper procedure going to test the food in the cafeteria when I grabbed the clip to get my paper to grade the food, I was looking down at it. The ADW of housing unit lady was standing in front of me. I had a table of COs eating next to us. The sergeant that was at the table just started yelling at the top of his lungs, "You, you, you!" I did not think that he was talking to me, so I looked behind me as if he was talking to one of the chow hall workers. He said, "No you," to me. He yelled, "Tame your eyes. Stop looking at that lady."

The whole chow hall stopped and was looking at me. I was embarrassed. The fact of matter was that I was not looking at that lady in no form or fashion. I was looking at my grade sheet, looking at what I was to grade for lunch. I could not say anything. The sergeant kicked me out of the chow hall. I walked out but would wait for him outside to get a better understanding. I know how COs worked; if he thought that I was looking that lady up, then I would get a ticket for it. After about a half hour, he walked out of the chow hall. I walked to him and told him that I was not looking at that lady. He told me not to worry about it and to go finish my lunch. That's when I knew that I was the butt of their joke. Truthfully, it just added to the fire of me wanting to find a way to leave that prison.

After a while, going over all my choices, I found that at that point, there were only two ways out of that prison. To find a way out through the warden's form or by just packing my things and walking to the control center, refusing to lock down. I did not like that option—for one, other inmates looked down on other inmates for locking up. So I would try to go through the warden's form. Besides, I was on my second term and would not be able to run again. So I had nothing to lose. I just needed to find a subject that was touchy with the administration and keep bringing that issue up. I also soon found out what it was that Eastside wanted of me. Because I went to chow with COs to test food, when the unit went to chow I would be back for the most part by myself. He would also stay back and rob others and a few times would have me to watch out. East Side knew that I did not want to do that, but he also knew that I was not going to tell him no. I had to play his game. What he did not know was that I was going to play it the way that I wanted to play, not how he thought I would. I knew some of the inmates he would be hitting. So behind his back and only to the ones I trusted, I told them what East Side did. At first, I was not going to do that to East Side, but my bunkie Mike helped me to put into proper perspective that what was right was right. Without Eastside knowing it, it was setting up for him to get a swift kick in his ass without him knowing it.

G was getting married soon; he told me that I would be the best man. I did think that was cool. But then at the last minute, while I was looking to get my hair done, trying to get an outfit, he switched up on me and had a different inmate go out there with him. I thought that was low of him. We stopped talking for a while because of that.

Chad was going home soon. Newell and I started hanging out a lot. We started sharing stories. He told me about the time he smoked crack and about his case, which was robbery. After hanging out with Newell for a while, I came to the thought that he was cool. I had never openly told anyone about me giving up John at MTU or about what happened to me at Bethany Creek. Something was different about Newell, so I told him everything. Since it was all done and could not be taken back, we laughed. The truth was that none of it was funny while I went through those events.

The next day, the prison next door to the one that I was at had a riot. No prison administration wants anything to do with their prison having a riot. People in the administration lose jobs, and after it was done, they did. The warden, among others that ran that prison, lost their jobs. That's when a light clicked in my head. I felt that I could use that to my advantage. On our warden's form, we had a loud mouth that always ran his mouth that openly rebelled against the administration. Somehow, I needed things to work in my favor to get me out of that prison. That day, before my unit counselor Ms. Flight left, I told her that I had some important info that the administration might want to know about members of the warden's form trying to start a riot. The next morning, first thing, I was called to the control center as if I needed to see a doctor. The warden assistant was there and wanted to know what I knew. I told him the same thing that I had told my ARVS, that members of the warden's form were trying to start a riot like the one that just happened next door. Since the administration already knew all the members of the warden's form, all I had to do was give them names. There were two inmates that I could not stand on the form. I gave up both their names. If I set the bait, the fish would bite. Everything needed to go right, or it could all go bad. I went to the block rep meeting and indirectly raised the issue of a riot and sticking together and whatnot. And like I thought, the two loudmouths took it and ran with it. Bait taken, all I was hearing the next day was talk from inmates here and there talking about something big about to happen. Things were going good as I needed word to get around that a riot was about to take place. The more inmates that knew about it, the more my word would be credible, and if the administration thought that I was telling the truth, then I would get what I wanted, which was a transfer. The good thing about trying to get a transfer was that it did not matter where I went. I did not need to go close to home anymore; Crissy and I had stopped talking. I had time to do. When I did not want to be at a prison any longer, this would be what I would do.

Things finally caught up with Eastside for stealing while everyone was at chow. I only told those that he hit that I knew so they would not tell on me for helping them. I did not see it coming, but the night I was sleeping, I woke up to the most horrifying man's screams that I ever heard in my life, truthfully speaking. It was so horrible that I put my head under the covers like I was a little boy, scared of the Boogeyman. A man by the name of Pete had caught East Side while he was sleeping with a lock and a sock. That's why I did not like sleeping in seven-man cubbs; things like this happen. Pete got away with hitting Eastside, but he knew that he would not be able to stay there without East Side getting back at him. So Pete locked up.

Meanwhile, things did start to heat up about the so-called riots about to take place. I needed word so the administration rats could get word to them that something was about to happen. I knew that things were going well when I started seeing COs with cameras on the yard, watching the unit reps including me. One of the two loudmouths that I had given up was pretty much lying low. The other was doing what I needed him to do, out and about, starting shit. About an hour later, an emergency block rep meeting was called, which by the way was never done. And an emergency count time was called. The loudmouth inmate that I had put out there for a pawn was taken to the hole for an NOI (notice of intent), which meant that basically, the administration couldn't prove anything but they think or know you did or about to do something. So they put you in the hole up to two years till an investigation is done. Everything was going just as I planned it. Before leaving the yard and speaking with other warden form reps, everyone knew that something was not right and that the administration had to know about the riot. For the most part, everyone thought that at the meeting that they were going to load all the reps up unto a bus and ride us all out; it had happened before.

The heads of the prison came into the room. Everyone knew that one of us was talking to the administration. Even though it was me, I played surprised that one among us would do such a thing.

The heads of the prison were definitely taking it very seriously. There were heads of the prison that never came to those meetings. Sergeant, Captain, the warden—they were all there. And for a moment, I started to think that maybe I had bitten off more than I could chew. The meeting took place, and I just shut my mouth and let the chairman and the warden's assistant talk. They basically came to an understanding that the warden's form was not orchestrating a riot. And since they had what they thought was their man (the inmate that they took to the hole), I guess maybe they did believe it was over. The meeting was ended. The only thing that I could do was wait and see if they would hold their word and ride me out.

I started telling the people that talked to that I would be leaving soon. Newell was the only one that knew the real reason. I started talking back to G and told him that I would be leaving soon. He did not want me to, especially after I told him the real reason I was leaving. I told G because I trusted him. I still was kind of upset about him not taking me to be his best man. But I realized that since I knew G, no matter what, I knew that he had my back. So I let bygones be bygones. Mike was upset about me going as well, and even though he was hands down my best friend at that time, he had some things going on the side with the Aryan nation. I did not hold that against him. I just looked at it for what is was, just like blacks looked to the nation of Islam or Sunni Muslim for protection when they came to prison. Unfortunately, it cost Mike to get his ass beaten.

One day, while trying to impress the leader one day on the yard, another member of the Aryan Brothers called him out on the yard. They went into the shack on the yard, fought, and Mike lost. When he came into the unit with a black eye, I said, "Damn, who hit you?" He tried to make me believe that it happened playing basketball, but I knew better. We left it at that.

I found out that Ms. P's vacation was coming to an end, and truthfully, I did miss our little conversations that we used to have or her picking on me. When she came back, I was all high on pills. I saw her for only a moment her first day back. It was when I went to the bathroom and we just simply crossed paths. It was pretty much like that on her second day as well. I only saw her when I walked to the bathroom. I saw her, she saw me, but we did not speak. I was too high off pills anyway. I could not have a conversation with her under the influence.

On her third day back, while walking to the bathroom, she yelled to me, "Why are you not talking to me? Say hi to me!" I thought that was crazy, I felt that she really wanted me to speak with her. Yet at the same time I would not try to get her friendliness confused with my personal feelings with her just being nice to me. I would stop taking the pills and sober up so that I would not sleep through her shift to speak with her.

The next day, I was 100 percent and looking forward to having a conversation with Mrs. P. I had to catch her at the right time. I also had to say the right words. Like I said earlier, I did not want to confuse her just being nice to me for something more than that. I caught her by herself later that day in the office. The other COs were on lunch break. I walked in and asked her if she would answer a few questions that stayed between us. She said yes, and I believed her, but I still would be smart about what I said and how I said things to her. In an indirect way, I described to her about me and a woman that I had feelings for, but because she worked in the administration, I was not allowed to share my feelings in the open. It was not allowed. I made sure that the things I described and talked about pointed straight at us. She came right back and asked a few questions of her own. She wanted me to put a name to her. I felt that she knew that I was talking about her, so I did not. Besides, I wanted her to know that I could be trusted after going back and forth with questions and answers. She said that she did not want to risk it with her job on the line. She said that if I was out and off parole, she would give it a try. I understood, thanked her for her time, and left it at that. I had not gotten any indication that I would be riding out, so I made up my mind that if I was not packed up and rode out the next few days, I was going to pack my things, walk to the control center, and refuse to lock down. I started getting my store in good shape so that I would be able to take a lot of good food with me. I told Will, Newell, G, and Mike all my goodbyes. Chad had gone home. G pretty much begged me to stay, 20 percent 'cause we were friends and the last

80 percent because I was giving him food. Every night, Mike went as far as to tell Hadler. Hadler did not believe him till Mike opened my locker and showed him that my things were packed and ready to go. Hadler made me unpack all my things, but that was not going to stop me.

CHAPTER FIFTEEN

STF

The next morning, I walked up to the control center at 8:00 a.m. The cool thing about it was that my unit COs that morning did not want to go through the work of going through my property, so before I left, he had me fill out the sheet of everything that I had, which meant that they would not go through my things and take out what I did not have my number on it. I walked into the control center and asked to speak with a sergeant. When he came, I told him that I was not going to be fighting so I had to lock down. I went through the normal procedure, with a counselor talking to me, trying to get me to tell some names of the people I feared my life from. I kept to my story and was told to sit tight. I would be leaving soon.

Just before my ride came, Mrs. P came to the control center. She opened the door and just looked at me. I had seen that look more than a few times on Crissy's face, so I knew what she wanted to say but did not. The only thing that I said was "You packed my things," as in she kicked me out of this home.

She said, "No, you packed your things." We smiled at each other. She walked out of my life.

About an hour later, I was taken next door to STF Middle Michigan prison facility. When I got next door as proper protocol, I seen the doctor, got my Quartermaster belongings, I was sent to

154

my unit, which was B Block. Like other prisons, when I got there, I stayed to myself and observed my surroundings to get a better understanding of the type of inmates I would be jailing with now. After getting my bed roll, I went to my cubb and started meeting my new cubbies. My bunkie's name was Rob; he was 375 pounds. Without him telling me what he had done to come to prison, I already knew. Child molestation. All he did was watch cartoons and other kid channels all day, and he was all right with it.

Across from us was Perry, which was not his real name. He was openly homosexual. That was his girl name, and that was all that I knew him by. His bunkie's name was Chief; that was not his real name. Since he was an Indian, that is what people called him.

On the other side were Sag Nasty and his Bunkie Black, both not their real names, just what they wanted to be called. Black was older and seemed cool. He and Perry were doing the most talking while I was in the cubb, telling me the dos and don'ts of the unit and the prison. And then there was Al. From looking at him, I would have guessed easy seventy-five years old. Someone that definitely should not have been in prison. Black made it his business to tell me Al's personal case out loud in front of the whole cubb. Al had worked at an old folks' home and got caught giving oral sex to one of the patients that he was supposed to have been bathing up. To add assault to it all, the patient had served his country in one of the wars. In his old age, he could not move or speak anymore. Blacked asked Al if he could go back and do anything differently, what would it be. Al said something, which totally shocked me cause the whole time up to that point, he had been quiet. He said that he would have locked the door so that he would have gotten away with what he was doing. I was at a loss for words.

After getting all my things together like unpacking and getting my bed made, I walked to the officers' station to request a cubb change. At that point, I did not have anything against anyone in the cubb that I was in. I just did not want to be in the observation cubb. It was loud from all the other different inmates yelling right next to my head. I wanted to get out of there. That was when I first saw the unit ARW, Ms. Jacks. Ms. Jacks was about thirty-five years old but one of the best-looking women that I had seen and been around in a long time. Every time she walked out of the office, inmates would stop just to watch her walk 'cause she did have a mean walk. Since I knew no one from this other prison yet and did not see anyone that I knew, I went back to my cubb and asked Black if he knew anyone that was from Muskegon in the unit. He told me that he did. He took me around to the back side of the unit and introduced me to Louis. Louis was about 6 feet, 4 inches easy, 250 pounds without any fat. He was from North Muskegon, which was cool at home, we were not far apart. We were bound to know some of the same people. I told him that I did not know many people form Muskegon 'cause I spent most of my time in Twin Lake. He then told me that there was someone from Twin Lake there. I told him to take me to him. We walked up the hallway and stopped at Robert's bunk. At first, when Robert stood up, I did not recognize his face. It had been so long since I had seen anyone from back home. We started talking, and I found that he was not too far from going home. I wanted to hit the yard and find more people that I knew, and since Robert was in the unit, I told him that we would talk later. I hit the yard and thought that it was sweet (considering that I had to be there). The layout of this prison was pretty much what an inmate would call wide-open. There was no yard correction officers, they had shacks where they would watch the yard from. They did have eyes in the sky but only two. I walked back to the weight pit to see how that layout was, and it was okay.

On my way back to the unit, I saw Gibbs from SPR. I walked up to him. We both were on our way back to the unit. We both laughed and hugged. I liked Gibbs, one of the only Mobits that I trusted and was cool with. After talking I found out that he was now the Grand Shrek (the leader of his religious organization). After walking the yard, talking, and catching up, he started introducing me to other homeboys that were there. If it were not for Gibbs, I would not have known anyone. There was little Dee that played basketball and was on Gibbs's team. He was my age, so that was cool. He would be someone I could kick it with if I had no one else. Gibbs introduced me to other homeboys that were from back home. Some even knew my family members. My brother had done time there, so a lot of people knew him as well. I soon found that the leader of our homeboys was a guy by the name of Pun. Once we got introduced, after walking away, I realized that I did not really care for him. There was just something about him that I did not like. There were other homeboys like Wonn who were over there from when he locked up. I kept it to myself about all the bullshit that he did to me. If I needed to, I would just use it as leverage.

Later that night, going back to my unit, I noticed something did not feel right. From level four and being in level two, being around all those prisoners with life, when something was about to happen, I learned to feel it in the air. So I sat on my bed and watched and listened. Sag Nasty, from what I was picking up, robbed a Mexican while the guy was sleeping. During third shift, he bear-clawed in the cubb across the hall, pulled out the foot locker, and took everything in there. I would never have the balls to try to pull something off like that myself. I thought Sag Nasty was crazy. So they just sat there, looking at each other. I guess the robbery took place the day before I came. By sizing Sag Nasty up, I could tell he knew how to handle his body weight well. He was my height but had way more muscle than me. Since the Mexican knew Sag Nasty robbed him, we just had to wait to see what happened.

While talking to Perry, he started telling me about the programs in the school and the general library. We started talking about books that we both had read that we both liked. I would not have talked to Perry outside our Cubbs. But from what I gathered about him, he was all right. He told me that the school had trade programs that one could use outside prison. He said that he knew the secretary and could get me into one of the classes. After looking into it and seeing everything they had, I choose electronics trade. I filled out a form and gave it to Perry. Perry then went into this long talk with me about how he was protected by the Mobits and all the other stuff. Then it hit me—the inmate that kept walking by our cubb must be Perry's boyfriend, and as sure as shit, he came to the door and started talking. His name was Chris. I did not know how true it was, whether the Mobits were or were not protecting Perry, but it was not unheard of. The truth was in secret or out in the open, most condoned homosexuality. Not Gibbs, so we would see what he thought about it.

The next day, I learned the warden form's last term was coming to an end. I thought it would be cool to get back into the nick of things. I had a few weeks to start to let people get to know me so that I could get the votes.

They did not fight, from what Sag Nasty told me; they just sat there—him and the Mexican—looking at each other all night. But this morning, the Mexican locked up. I talked with Sag Nasty a little to try to get to know him a little better. We found that we were about the same age and that he was in prison for strong armed robbery, go figure. I instantly put it out there to him but—but in an indirect way toward him—that if anyone took anything from me, I would hit him with a lock and a sock. I told him that with the time that I had left, I had nothing to lose, so I did not care. After that conversation, we became cool and had an understanding.

I went to the yard and started talking to Gibbs. He told me that after all the years that he had been in prison, he finally got his parole. I was happy for him. Gibbs had been in prison for over twenty-five years. It was his time. In a joking manner, I told Gibbs that I wanted him to know but did not want him to say anything about what I told him concerning the things Perry had said about being protected by the MO's not being a member, with respect to Gibbs, he did not know my experiences with MO's were bad. Gibbs was very different with a lot of respect anything I addressed with him that was wrong. I hated the Mobits, but he and I were so cool that whenever I saw the Mobitz do something that I did not like, I could say something to him about it and it would stay between us. No big deal, so I told him what Perry said. I had nothing against Perry and did not want to get him or his boyfriend in trouble. It was more of I knew that Gibbs as the leader of all those people that was not acceptable as Gibbs did not keep it to himself. It did not take long for it to get hot and heated. I asked Gibbs not to say anything, but he did. He made me say everything that I told him in front of Chris. I was a little upset knowing that's how fights got started, but I also knew that Gibbs was leader of his crew, and his word was final. It ultimately came down to Chris not being allowed to go to service anymore. That was his choice, he picked Perry over the Mobits, even though I did not want to be involved with doing that I did have a profound even more respect for Gibbs. He was one of the few Mobits with power that I knew that did not use it the wrong way. I told him about a guy in my cubb, Sag Nasty, whom I feared would rob me. Gibbs said that was his family from the street. We gave Sag Nasty a door call. Gibbs told him that I was his family to not let nothing happen to me. I knew I did not have to worry about him robbing me. While walking the yard, I saw one of my old cubbies from Pine River. In the last prison, it was Mickey that used to give me all the pills. Now he was over here, he told me that he had the amount of pills they gave him, and if I wanted some I would first on his list. He told me where he locked at. I told him that I would get with him later when I found all the other homeboys. I saw that they were with some nation of Islam boys, so something was on the floor. I waited off from a distance. After both parties went their own way and I caught up with Pun and the other homeboys, I learned that Wonn had run up a bill, that he could not pay with the Nation brothers wanted either their money or his head. But since Wonn was from Muskegon, and there was so many of us from there. They had to go through Pun since he was supposedly the leader of all our homeboys. To do anything harmful to Wonn, they had to first talk to Pun. From my understanding, Pun ended up paying the bill of debt Wonn owned, and Pun was going to take Wonn under his wings. I knew that Wonn was trouble, but I knew or felt that it was not my place to tell them that Wonn was trouble, so I let it pass. I went to the yard and found a guy that was selling spud juice on the yard. It had been a while since I got drunk, so I thought, *Why not?* I had a locker and foot locker. Full of money, I was told how the prison was flooded with all kind of different drugs. One could get almost anything if one knew the right people. That's what the inmate told me. He didn't just want to come out and say that he was selling drugs 'cause he did not know me and I did not know him. When I started telling him who I was and who my people were, we came to an understanding that I was cool. He told me that he had pills, weed, heroin, and spud juice.

I brought a dime of weed and two bottles of spud. I could get with Mike later if I needed some pills. I did want to do heroin but did not want to do it alone, so I would wait. I pretty much kept to myself for the rest of the day. While sitting in my bed the next day, I started to realize that I had not been talking to anyone from back home—my mom, brothers, or sister. Even Crissy. I did think about her and my son time to time, but even if I wanted to write her, I could not 'cause when we had our last fight, she did not let me know where she was going. And besides that, I had been told for years that the day I let the streets go and focus on doing my time, then my time would start to go by fast. Truthfully, I can say time was going by good and fast for me. On yard that day, I started noticing other people that were coming from next door prison. Heavy's brother, he was there; he was on TV, the Detroit DEA show. I remembered seeing him. The funny thing was that I watched that whole show. He was one of the only ones on that Detroit DEA show that had gotten caught. He did not snitch to get out of doing the time. We talked a little, and I learned that his brother Heavy from SPR did go home. I told him that we would get together later. Polo was there. He was in my unit. They just did a random move with him and another inmate. He said G was still next-door doing the same thing that he was doing when I left, going on visits with his newly wife while working out in the weight pit. Robert would be leaving soon so I spent time with him most of that reminiscing about home. Calling home the other day, He said they were saying I was a homosexual, Robert let me know, he took up for me as he knew that was not true. all I could do at that point was agree with him because I was not. I had a bad experience at Bethany Creek that spun out of control, not good getting back to the streets. I Denied Everything that was said about me, at the same time also knew that one day I would have to deal with it.

After a few days, Robert left and he went home. I woke up one morning to Black and Chris arguing. I was mad that I woke up to their loud mouths. I was not going to say anything so, I just listened to what they were going back and forth about. I guess Black was upset about Chris walking into our cubb without letting anyone know. Black earlier had, out of respect, asked Chris to stop doing that. But since Chris and Perry were involved and Chris kept food in Perry's locker. I guess that he felt he was entitled to walk into our cubb as he pleased. With all fights in prison, one thing lead to another. Things were said in front of people that can't be taken back, and punches got slung. Before they stopped fighting, the police came out of the office and caught them fighting. They were taken to the hole. Everyone thought it was funny how Perry was yelling like a girl, "Stop, Chris." I thought it was funny too.

Later that day, I was called to the school for a reason. At the time, I did not know the reason, but I went. When I got over there, I was asked if I was still looking to get into electronics trade class. I said yes and was told I would start the next day or so. I also was told to watch the system for my name. When I walked back to the unit, even though Perry did not want to see or speak with anyone, I had to thank him for pulling strings and helping me get into classes. As long as I had been in that unit, I did not see much of my homeboys. Louis, I did pass him time to time coming from the weight pit or the chow hall. I really did not see much of him. I was also told by the other homeboys just how he was. For the most part, he did not mess with others. He just kept to himself. Today, I thought I would walk around and see how he was doing. He told me he got our local newspaper if I wanted to look at them every day. I thought that was okay. So I would start making it a priority to start kicking it with Louis. Besides, he was big as hell. If shit hit the fan, which I was sure it would, I wanted to start a store again. It would be good to have a homeboy like Louis on my side.

There was an inmate from around the unit named Freddy. He was my age. At first, we would talk about shows that we both liked to watch on TV. One thing led to another overtime. We became pretty cool with each other. Block reps' vote was to be held that day as well. I had been in the unit long enough to let people for the most part see me. Being in the first cube helped as well. To get to the lobby, they passed us, so for the most part, everyone or a lot of people knew of me. Like I said before, the warden's form was mostly a popularity contest. What I did have going for me that was good a lot of people voted by prison number as well. I was surprised to see that on the back side, I had the oldest number. I had been down for over little more than six years, but my number was not considered a fish number any longer. I was not old school either, so I would just have to wait and see how it went. I started feeling real good when I heard Freddie and the other cubbs around me start to say I had their votes. Later that day, after the vote, I found that I was the new unit block rep. Ms. Jacks, my unit counselor, called me, and the white rep, into her office. For the most part, she told us what she expected out of us and that she wanted to have monthly meetings to bridge the gap between inmates and her staff and make it all fine and agreeable. I liked Ms. Jacks; she was cool and funny as hell. My first order of business was to become the food rep. There was not much I had to do but go to the monthly meeting and eat good. I would just have to wait and see. So I started school, which was okay. I thought that it was going to be class, that the teacher would sit in front of the class and teach. That was not the case. All throughout, the teacher did talk a lot, when we first came in. Then he would sit down, and we had to go at our own pace. Everyone else in the class seemed to be going at their work well. I didn't understand any of it quite honestly. I found myself at the teacher's desk most of the day. I felt like I was being talked down to instead of being helped. After a while, smoke break was called. There was the white guy; he seemed cool. I walked over to him and found that he was having the same problems that I was having with the bookwork. The difference between him and me was that he knew an inmate that had taken the class before us. He had all the answers to the questions. I told him if it was all right, I wanted to go with him to look into it as well. I knew that I was having a hard time with it the first day. First lesson, I knew that the class was going to be hard. The inmate said I could just call him Old School. After class, we walked over and found the guy that had all the questions to the answers. He also had all the answers to all the tests. As long as we did not get caught, we were going to turn a two-year course into a six-month course. Since I was in the unit, Old School had me hold all the answers, which was cool. Later that day, I went to my first block meeting with my fellow inmates. I became the food rep again. I truly did not do many things. I just wanted to eat but soon found it was not done over here as it was done over there. We did not test the food, so I would not be eating like I did at the last prison.

Later that day, after walking the yard, I saw Old School off by himself sitting under a tree. I went over to talk to him. We started talking about home, women, and drugs. I found out that Old School smoked a lot of weed, took pills, and smoked heroin. He was on it right then and there. I can't stand when people blow my high, so kindly I walked off and told him that I would catch him tomorrow at school. So that's what I did for the most part for a while—went to school, took pills here and there. When I was not doing that, I would read on the yard, be at the library, or work out. I got myself into that kind of a routine. I felt that I was on a college campus. I mean I never went to school outside high school. But that's all we did—I went to school all day then we partied. The only thing we did not have was women. It was honestly starting to take a toll on me. Doing time, being locked up, and doing it alone it was hard. I needed a friend but had burned all my bridges. I would have to weather the storm. I did like all my older homeboys there, but with the age difference, we really did not have much to talk about. So unless all the homeboys were out and about watching a basketball game or something, other than that, I never hung out with any of them. D Dozer was cool and we were the same age, but I never hung out with any of them like I thought we would. The fact was I felt bad vibes coming from Pun, and he was the leader of all the homeboys. They looked to him and while kissing his ass. Not because they loved, liked, or respected him. It was because they feared him from the shit that he used to do back home all those years ago. Or like the young ones that had been kids when Pun was out there, the stories were told. I just decided for the most part to just keep to myself and only deal with a few homeboys from home. Besides, it was not like I was jailing at a prison like MTU or Bethany Creek or anything like that. I did see someone get hit with a lock in a sock in the yard. By the way, that was crazy. You know I fought here and there, nothing out of control. It was a few weeks later that one of my unit COs came to wake me up to tell me that today I was moving to the backside of the hallway. I thought that would be cool; Louis was back there. I wanted to start my store, but in order to do that, I needed to move, and I got what I was look-ing for. I also was moving to the back. Every store, Sag nasty would take Al's whole store bag. I felt bad a little, but every time I thought about what he did on his case, those feelings would go away. While in the process of moving, Eastside from next door was moving into our unit as well the inmate from the last prison that hit him while he was sleeping was in our unit I thought to myself this was going to be entertaining to watch unfold since I was cool with East side and on speaking terms with the other guy that hit him I told Eastside first that the inmate that hit him while he was sleeping with that lock in the sock was in the back hallway. So I gave him (Eastside) a heads up. Like I said, though I was not overly cool with the inmate that had hit Eastside, we were on speaking terms, so I would give him word before Eastside could get to him. I knew that since it was early, noth-ing would go down till later, so I had time.

I went to the new cubb to unpack my things. I had been in the unit long enough by now to know who was who by this time. Having been in the unit as long as I have and being the block rep, I felt that if I did not personally know you, then I had seen you around. That was not the case with my new cubb. The first one that I found when I walked in was Brock, a bald-headed older black man from Detroit. Everyone else in the cub was sleeping. So after telling me about him-self, he told me the rest of my cubby's names. The two across from us were Buzz, he was a Indian, and his bunkie's name was Cookie. That was not his real name, just one he went by. I had seen him around the prison time to time. All he did was go to chow and play tennis. He was older and kept to himself. On the other side across from us was Slightent Bob. Most people called him Slight Shit just to pick on him; quite frankly he was nasty as they come. I did not know him either, just seen him around time to time. He used to go around and pick up old rolled-up cigarettes and smoke them. He also walked around behind COs when they smoked to pick up their cigarettes; he was nasty. His bunkie was a tall black man named Tom. Tom was always mad and had an attitude, so he kept to himself—well, that's how Brock my bunkey thought of him. The last two bunks belong to a homosexual named Dave. I did not know Dave, he used to always come around my old cubb to talk to Perry. That how I knew he was homosexual. I did not have anything against it. I just did not want to be labeled wrong. So if we talked, I would keep it short. He did not have a bunkie, but one was coming. It was still early, so I put all my things away so I could go to school. Later that day, I had a block rep meeting at which something very important was going to be told to us. So everyone was looking forward to that.

At school, Old School and I were doing well. We had rented that paperwork and were flying through the class. The only thing that we were having problems with was hands-on parts. We did not have paperwork on how to read schematics, so that part we would have to learn. We were moving at the same pace, so they made us partners, which was very beneficial for both of us. Again, while off by ourselves, he told me that a package was coming in later with some heroin, and he asked me if I would want to do some. For years I had been interested but never had the balls to try it. I also did not want anyone else to know. From what I had seen and really known about Old School, I felt that he could be trusted. So I asked him when he was going to get the goods. He told me to meet him on the yard tonight at about 7:30 p.m. I told him okay and said that I did not want to shoot it. He did not like that idea, but I did not like the idea of sharing needles. Needles are hard to come by. So after agreeing with me, he just gave me some to snort.

After school, when I got back to my own cubb, everyone was up and about. Even the inmate from down the hall that had hit East Side with that lock in a sock. I stopped him walking to the bathroom to let him know East Side got moved over to our unit this morning. And I wanted to give him a heads up. He said he was not worried, but his face showed something else. After count time, we would just have to see. I had to go to my block rep meeting after count to see what this important news was being told to us today. I did not want to leave if shit went down. After count, they both went into the day-room, one by one, not together. I watched them talk, but nothing happened. If East Side was going to do something, he would not have talked. So I left to the block rep meeting, I would find out about what it was they talked about later. I arrived at the meeting with my fellow members of the warden's form. Nobody had heads up on what it was about or what was going to be said; all we could do was wait and see. When the Warden walked in with two more from his administration. He said that a new deal had been done with a different health care program. The prior one, we had now had gotten outbid and lost their contract. The bad news about that part of the new deal with the new health care was they wanted the MDOC to remove all tobacco products off the stores. COs and inmates were no longer allowed to smoke or have cigarettes on their person. So the COs were affected by this as well. The warden was not telling us to fight this issue; we were being told so that we could pass the word as a warden form to keep the shit down. We quickly argued that was not our place. We were only the voices to speak for the population. Some good news that came from the bad news was that they were not going to make us go cold turkey. Tobacco had a time limit of eight months to be out of the system. So what they was going to do was every store until that date that had tobacco had to be out of the system. They were going to start to limit how much we would be able to buy. No one believed that this would hold up. There were going to be a lot of level two and four inmates that would be affected by this. Our warden Nick said he had gone to a wardens' meeting with other wardens across the MDOC, and they were expecting everything, even riots. This was a major change in policy, and a lot of people were going to be affected, and they wanted to give us the block reps' heads up before the memos went out. I was not really a smoker, so I was not worried about it. I did smoke when I got high; that was mostly Black and Milds. I left that meeting knowing that a lot of shit was going to start going down. About the cigarettes, chewing tobacco, and Black and Milds. Prices were going to skyrocket, which would lead to fights, riots, stealing, and all other kinds of bullshit.

When I get back to the unit and finally found East Side, I learned that the inmate that had hit him worked things out and came to some kind of understanding. None of which had anything to do with me, so I left it alone. Me and the other unit rep started telling others about tobacco being taken out of the store. Some did not believe, others did not care, and some just talked shit. I was only the messenger, so that's what I did; I told them what was told to me. Like the warden had said, later on that day, the memos were put up. The memos said that the next eight to eleven months, they were going to limit how much tobacco would be sold per inmate. Then they gave us the rundown, that from now on until it had to be gone. We could only buy four pouches or items per store this month; matches and papers counted as an item. As the month went down, so did the number of tobacco items that we could get. By the eighth month, tobacco products would stop selling all together. They would give us the following next three months to have all tobacco products out of the system. If not one would be subject to a substance abuse ticket.

When I arrived back at my cubb, I saw that we had a new cubby. He introduced himself as Raw Raw. I thought to myself, the vibes I got from him were good. I asked him if it was okay that I called him Raw, even though I knew that wasn't his real name. Is it all right if I just call him Raw? He said that would be cool. After count time, I went to Louis's cubb, which was right across the hallway from mine. I kicked it with him for a while. I did like Louis. I knew that if we did become cool, if shit hit the fan, he had my back. After chow lines, we were going to come back and show each other pictures to see if we knew each other. Honestly, my mind was focused on what was going down that night. When I was to catch up with Old School, I was looking forward to doing heroin for the first time. In the past, I had heard so many people talk about it. When I went to rehab and seen the effects it had on people there, I told myself I was not never going to do that drug. It's funny how time passes and we forget such things. After getting back from chow lines and going over pictures with Louis, I did not know or recognize anyone in his pictures. Just like him, we both had brothers locked up. He also did not know anyone from my pictures. He said he had a few more I did not see. When he came back, they were pictures of him and the mother of his child. She looked familiar, but I could not put a name or memory of her face. I also did not want to be rude and ask questions. I did ask Louis what school she did go to, and just like I thought, Rockets. The same school that I went to. I told him that I knew a girl with the same name as hers. That went to Reeth Puffer and my mom's church;

she was a Mormon. He said that was her. I knew the mother of his child as well. We use to make out in the backwoods of the church while service was going on. She was fine as hell. Of course, I would never tell Louis about that. I could tell by the look in his eyes, even though at that time, he was mad at her for not being there. The way he wanted her to be there. The truth was that he loved the women. Louis asked if I wanted to start working out with him and his crew. As much as I did, I also did not want to hold them up. I knew that they all were stronger than me. So I would just end up slowing them down. Louis told me not to worry about it, since the next two days were their days off o working out. He said that he would talk to the crew and make sure it was all right and to take me out with them later. Before we went our separate ways, another homeboy from home started talking to us. He said that they called him Gamble; he was older. I did not know any of his people, and he did not know any of mine. Gamble ran one of the biggest stores in the unit but was going home soon. So he was starting to slow down. He told me that if I needed anything to just come down and holler at him. I would, not because I needed anything. I just wanted to know he was true for his word.

Later that day, I went to the backyard and found Old School under the tree that he always sat, under where we agreed to meet. He kept his word; he had over a hundred in prison value of heroin, which by the way was not considered a lot. After I sat down, he gave me two lines to snort. He told me to do it in my unit bathroom just in case I had to vomit. It was common with most people after doing it. It would only happen in the beginning. So I went to the bathroom with a magazine, made two lines, and snorted heroin for the first time. After throwing up, I remember going back to my room to enjoy the high, but I kept nodding out. I felt sleepy yet at the same time aware what was going on around me. I felt good; the feeling was too good.

The next day at school, I told Old School about the experience that I had. He told me that he always had it, that if I wanted to do more, he was my guy. He did make it known that he was not going to support my habit. If I wanted to ride the train, I had to buy my own bus ticket, which I respected. On my way back to the unit from school that day, I saw a guy that I knew from one of the other prisons. When I was at Carson City, his name was Byron. Byron was talking to an inmate that I did not know. But he was in my unit; we walked in together. Talking to him, I learned that he was from Flint, and that's what he wanted to be called. I had a good friend that I knew from a different prison, Bethany Creek from Flint. His name was Little Bob. Little Bob was a straight up killer from Flint, Michigan, caught his case when he was fifteen, murder. I had also done time with Little Bob at MTU. I asked Flint if he knew Little Bob. He said he did, and before Little Bob had caught his case and gone to prison, they had been best friends. They were still cool to this day. I had personally seen Little Bob put in work. So for Flint to say that they were friends and still talked meant a lot. Flint told me that he locked in the same cubb as my homeboy Gamble. So I knew that we would get to know each other better. I did want to get to know my cubbies a little better to see who I could trust. I wanted to get my store off the ground because I had no other kind of income coming in. Drugs, personal hygiene, and eating would start to add up. I learned fast that Buzz (the Indian) went to the store for one hundred. Every store, most of it, if not all of it, was going to the store man. I needed to bring him in fast. I saw him; he was already dealing with someone. So in order to get in good with him, I would have to backdoor the guy that he was already dealing with. My bunkie was cool, older, and always trying to talk. He was studying to be a drug counselor. So the things he would read from the book, he would share with me, in part because he knew that I was truthfully listening. Truthfully, sometimes, it was good to hear the things that he used to tell me. But then other times, he outdid himself because it seemed like he never wanted to stop talking. I would never be rude and tell him that. For the most part, Raw, my bunkie Brock, and Buzz would be the only ones that I messed with. I did find Silent Bob funny, but he was just a nasty man.

Later that day, Louis came got me to introduce me to some of his workout crew. Nrad was one of them; he locked in the first cubb down the rock. I did not know him, but he seemed cool. He told me that he did not mind me working out with them as long as I did the workouts and did not quit. I was strong for my size, so I thought to myself that would not be a problem. Louis took me outside and introduced me to Wise and Sam, the other workout partners, as well. They were older and from different units, so the only time that I would see them would be in the Weight Pit. They were both older, so it was not like I would be hanging out with them. So I got into a normal daily program. On weekdays after school, I would hang out with. Raw, Sag Nasty. Flint came around sometimes with us. He thought that Raw was homosexual; I did not see it. But if he was, those were his boundaries and had nothing to do with me. So I never said anything. I also spent a lot of time with Freddy. We would drink and take pills together. Old School from school and I kicked it here and there. His drug of choice was heroin, and I liked the feeling too much. I tried to limit my time with him to just school and smoke breaks. When all else failed, I would get me a book and read. I still wrote in my daily journal but not like I once did. I also for the most part stopped going to Buddhist services. Reading fantasy books is what I did in my free time. The homeboys used to think that I was crazy. I use to lie under a tree and read. I guess I was different.

CHAPTER SIXTEEN

The Store

A few months later, I happened to be sitting in my unit's dayroom, and Newell walked through the door. I could not believe it was the third prison that he and I were in together. Next door at the last prison before I left, we had started to get cool. Newell knew the truth about all I did at the other prisons, so I would have to bring him in and keep him close. The first thing I told him was to go unpack and get himself situated, come out and meet me, and I would take him to meet some of the homeboys. That's what I did—took him around the unit to the few homeboys in the unit then took him outside to the followers of Pun. They would relate to Newell better than to me. Newell was from the same hood. I was from the outskirts, so no one paid me any mind for the most part, and I was okay with that. While taking Newell around, I caught up with him on some news about the last prison. I also learned that Newell was going to be seeing the parole board soon. So he was getting ready to go home. By now, I knew the right people to get Newell into school if he wanted to, and he did. I got him in the building trades a few weeks later. It was important for him to get into his own daily program. I had mine, and when I was into it, I did not want to be bothered. Everyone knew that when I was not at school, I would read fantasy books. When I did not do either of those, I would work out and hang out with

Newell and friends. Get high or drunk. As I said before, it was like a college campus. For some odd reason, that's silly way of thinking was making the time go by fast. Believe it or not, I was not talking to anyone from back home. Time was lost to me. Prison was my world. I eventually talked Newel into investing money into my store. I needed money to make money. By now, the little food (money) that I brought with me from the last prison was eaten or used on drugs. I seen how Buzz was spending his money crazy so I tried to get him to invest in the store. Newell was going to do it 'cause he wanted to be nice and not tell me no. Since he would be going home soon. He did not want the bullshit that came with running a store while pitching the idea to Newell and Buzz about the store. I let it be known that if anything ever went down, then I would be on the front line. They would not have to fight. Buzz gave me the okay. But I still knew that he was not yet committed. I would still have to work on him. He had too much money coming in for me not to get a piece of it.

The following day, Newell did start to invest into the store. It was slow but it was doing fine. One of our problems was that most of the time, we were smoking weed. That was starting to cost a lot. I started smoking cigarettes again. It started off at first with just Black and Mild cigars. But the more I smoked them, it started to add up. I was picking up a habit when they were about to take the tobacco from us. The whole time, my bunkie stayed on me. When he saw good, he would tell me to build on it. He would hit me hard on the bad. Sometimes I thought that he would never stop talking. The fact of the matter was that the things that he was telling me were true. He never lied to me, so most of the time against what I wanted to do. I would just sit there and listen. Later, RawRaw packed up, refused to lock down, and tried to leave the prison. They gave him a flop; he would have to stay in prison for twelve more months. For them not enrolling him into class that he needed to go home. Before, he walked up front he told me that he thought that I was cool and wanted to keep it real with me. He told me that he liked boys. Truthfully, I was stunned, but I would not judge him. If that was what he was into, it was on him. I expressed to him that he was still cool with me and that I hoped everything worked out for him. He left later that day, after count when the yard opened. I went outside to a door call and it was Raw Raw. I asked him why he was still here. "I thought you locked up." He said that they had promised to put him into the class he needed if he went back. The bad thing that came out of it was he would not be able to lock into my unit anymore. He was now in a different unit, which was fine. I would still be able to see and talk with him. He also would be able to get into the class he needed in order to go home. Against my better judgment, I went back and told Flint and Sag Nasty about Raw Raw. Sagnasty was kind of upset, I guess he felt that he was betrayed. Flint felt that he already knew so it was not surprise or a big deal. When I told them we were all right with each other, so I felt it was justified to tell them.

After a while, I started seeing that Newell and I were just keeping the store at a standstill or losing more than we were bringing in from drinking and all the smoking. So reluctantly, I talked him into having his mom send me some money toward our store and the little money that he had invested it all to get the store popping. Newell made it happen. I had a lockerful; he did as well. Everything was starting to go well. A homeboy rode in by the name of Roman. I did not know him, but I did know his sister. He knew some of the same people I knew, that was cool. Later that day, Newell and I were given a door call from Pun and a few other homeboys. We were told to watch Roman. He testified on another homeboy and got him life. My personal thoughts were it was one thing to tell on someone but a whole different thing altogether to get caught telling. I told myself I would deal with him with a long silver spoon. Later, he started asking for store goods, and I dealt with him against my better judgment. I kept the store items at a low. The bad thing was that he locked in the cub with Newell. So it was not like we could say no. He knew when we were out or when we had things in the store. Something in my gut told me not to mess with him; something was not right. A few stores later, he proved my bad feelings about him were correct. He did not pay me or Newell the money he owed us. I was not overly mad or surprised. Running a store, you take a loss here and there—that is just the way it is. When someone does not pay, I just don't give them anything else till they do. It's just one of my rules.

Roman played poker, so he needed money, but I was not going to break rules that had helped my store stay good. For as long as I'd been running store. So when he came to me asking for store goods when he still owned me, before I could even say that I was not going to give him anything 'cause he still owed me. I knew that it was going to be a problem. And it was later that day after lunch while I was sitting on my bunk with a cold. So I did not want to be bothered. Newell came and told me he had been robbed—the $75 food bag was gone. The rules of prison said that without proof, I could not do anything. So the first thing I did was start asking around of who might have seen anything that did not look right. For the most part, no one spoke up 'cause they knew that they would be dragged into something that had nothing to do with them. I respected that 'cause I had been in similar situations. I started telling all my homeboys, so if shit went down, people would have my back. Sag Nasty was there for me, Flint, Louis, and a few others. No one would make a move unless I did. The problem was I did not have any hard proof against anyone. Later that night, Freddy pulled me to the back hallway and said someone wanted to speak with me. When I got to the back, an inmate that I had seen around the unit here and there, no one I personally knew. He said he had seen Roman, just like I, had expected carrying a bag down the hallway. Around the same time, I got robbed. His statement was all I needed for proof. The problem was he did not want involvement. I needed him to tell Roman what he told me: no matter how much I needed him to speak up, he would not. I truthfully did not blame him. We both knew if he did, shit was going to come his way. As the night progressed, other pieces started to come together. I found out that Roman did not act alone. Another inmate from the front named Pell and the inmate that locked in the cubb across the hall from me named Black. Bell was approximately my size, black and from Pontiac. I was not worried about him or his homeboys. I was concerned about Roman. For one, he was a homeboy who locked in the same cubb as Newell. So if we fought, we would have to make him leave the compound after the fight. Worst scenario was that he was a Muslim, a prison religion, or gang, whatever you want to call it. He had some power behind this bullshit. Malantics, just like Mobits, condoned certain bullshit. So in order to fight Roman, which I had intended to do, I had to go through his chain of command. I felt this was the way to do it. This would keep some of the bullshit down without this going overboard. Others would have then acted differently, even though Newell and I got robbed. Others looked at it like it was Newell's locker that got robbed. So he would have to be on the front line, not me. Anything else people would look at as if I were fighting a white boy battle. One could easily turn this into a black and white issue. I decided to comfort Roman first. I pulled him aside alone. I told him what someone had told me, and he denied being any part of it. While in the bathroom talking with him, Newell came in. Other inmates that knew that Roman had robbed us came from nowhere, the leader of the Malantics. He and I agreed if I could get someone to confirm that he had seen Roman carrying my bag, that he himself would pay for everything. I did know the inmate that told me that he had seen Roman was not going to speak up. If he did, the $75 of merchandise that they took from us would end up coming from him for getting himself involved. I was not going to have that. I had some decisions to make, but first, I would talk to my closest friends or inmates that I kicked it with to get their point of view on this situation. The first person I spoke about this with was Baxter. He was all right and from the nation of Islam. So I knew his point of view would be based off prison politics. I felt I needed that. It was coming down, from the looks of this, that we were going to jump Roman. So I wanted to hear from Baxter how he thought the Malantics would take something like this. After giving me his opinion, I moved on and talked to Pun. He gave me no good feedback. Freddy, he told me, no matter what he had my back. Louis walked me on the yard with Nard. I was told by Nard that he knew the leaders of the Malantics on the compound. He was taking me to him now. When we all got together, he told me that he knew what Roman did. Regardless, Roman was not to get jumped or stabbed. If we wanted to fight, it had to be one on one. I told him okay and that Newell would fight Roman tonight; it was on. I went back to the unit and told Newell what was to go down.

The agreement was after count when the COs did their round. Newell was going to fight Roman. I knew with the size difference Newell probably had no chance, so I told him I would run down and help as soon as I heard noise from the fight. I did not care at this time what the Malanics was talking about or told us. I made up my mind to jump Roman. One thing I had learned about prison over the years was if there was another inmate that stole from you or wronged you and didn't respond that everyone would do it. They would think it was all right by now. Everyone knew that Newell and I had gotten robbed. Inmates were waiting to see how we would react. Around count time, my bunkie was trying to talk me out of doing anything that he thought I would regret. Truthfully, my mind was made up. I justified this with myself, reminding myself I still had a lot of time to do. I wanted respect. Prison stories stuck around for a long time. If we beat these boys, we would earn our respect. While the COs did their rounds, I waited for Newell to start fighting. So I could run down there. As time continued, I never heard the noise from fighting. I got madder every second that went by. My bunkey did not know that I was waiting to run down the hall to fight. So I finished listening to him talk. After count time cleared, I anxiously waited for Newell to come up the hall. To tell me what had happened. He told me that other inmates got robbed all the time and nothing never happens to them. He was right except the part where they lost respect. I knew what it was Newell was going home. He did not want to do anything jeopardize or prolong his parole. Out of anger, I told him to get the hell away from me. I went and had a conversation with Freddy about it. After a while of talking I realized that I should not have acted that way toward Newell. I had promised Newell if things came to this, I would be the front line, not him. I made up my mind by this time, that I would fight two of them that robbed us. Newell entered the dayroom, where I expressed to him that I should not have talked to him in that manner. I also did respect that he wanted to go home, that he did not want anything to do with fighting. While I was speaking to Freddy, Newell was on the phone with his mom, telling her everything. He asked me if I would speak to her over the phone. I did not know Newell's mother and did not have any idea why she wanted to talk with me. Reluctantly, I agreed. I did not know from Newell talking to me about his mom that she was a church woman. So if Newell informed her that we were going to fight; obviously, she would be against the violence. When talking to her, I found out that Newell had informed her of our situation. She was trying to talk me out of doing anything. I had to be careful of the things that were said over the phone. So I tried to get off the phone as soon as possible. I told her I was going to go do what I had to do, that I did not expect Newell to do anything. She knew that it was three inmates. I proclaimed to her that I was going to get at least two. She asked me if I thought I was a bad ass or something. Again, I told her I would do what I had to do and got off the phone. I made up my mind that the next morning, I was going to get Bell and Black the one my size and the white one locked across from me.

The next day, after a long morning of school, I was ready to fight. I got back to the unit from school. It was about ten minutes from count, I watched Bell buying Black and Milds with money, the money that I knew belonged to Newell and me. This just added fuel to the fire. I walked down to the restroom. Bell was there. He had no idea what I wanted and was capable of doing at that very moment. I held back; it was close to count time. After count, Newell came to me and said that he was willing to fight. I was shocked by him but went with it. I told him to fight Black, the white guy across the hall from me. He was sleeping at this time. In this situation, most inmates would have started to fight while he was sleeping. I told Newell that we would wait until he woke up so everyone could see us coming. I did not want to sneak them just like they did us. I told Newell to go back to his cell and remove some of his clothes. Since dude was bigger, I did not want him to rag doll Newell. When Newell got back, I told him not to let Black grab him. This would not be good. In eight-man cubbs, inmates did not go into other inmates' cubbs to fight. It was not allowed, mostly out of respect. I went to whom I believed was the leader of the cubb and told him. Also asked him for permission for Newell to go in his cubb to fight. JB, the inmate that I was talking to, said he had heard about what Black and others did. That it was all right for us to take care of what we needed to take care of. That was all I needed. Black woke up. I told Newell to go do his thing. He ran in the cubb, while Black was folding his sheets and went right to it. Honestly, I was impressed with what Newell was doing. He was punching Black in the face, slamming his back into the wall. Everything was going well. People started looking over the wall and up and down the hall. Then Newell got grabbed into a choke hold. I told him not to let that happen. All the good he did at first was going out the window. He started screaming and yelling, "Get him off me!" He was poking my eyes. I was pissed. We had a show to put on. I felt as though he was messing it up. Before I could intervene, I yelled, "Newell, get up! Do this, do that!" Newell gave up. I went into the cubb and told Black that it was over. At first, he did not want to stop, he must have heard the seriousness in my voice. The next time, I spoke and told him that it was over; he let Newell go. When they got up, Black's face was messed up bad from the earlier punches that Newell got in. I told Newell when he got up to go clean himself off; he had blood everywhere. Then I saw Bell coming up the hallway to check on Black, it was my turn. There was still a crowd. So I would be able to put on a show and make up for what Newell did. I told Bell to leave. I knew that he played a part of robbing Newell and me. He told me to miss him with that bullshit. I told him that he was not ready. He again repeated himself. I took it from there from the first punch to the last. Bell had nothing coming. I punched him in the face. I grabbed the back of his neck in order to keep control. I slammed him and picked him up in order to slam him again. I remember the crowd around me, cheering me on. It felt good. I remembered slamming Bell against the walls. He took a step back and tried to punch me in the face. I ducked, slammed him to the ground again, and mounted him. I told him you have nothing coming with me and punched him hard in the face, for time measure. I got up and went into my cubb. Bell was discombobulated, when he got up sluggishly trying to fight again. I started to give him exactly what he was looking for until the COs walked up the hallway. Someone told me they went right to Black's cubb and told him to go to the control center. They also directed Newell and myself among others to go to the control center as well. It was a total of six of us that had to report to the center. Bell was the only one who did not get called to report at control center, which was cool because his face was messed up the most. Someone was going to receive an assault ticket before this was over. I would and could only hope that no one would tell. I would be the last one to see the inspector; this was the only good thing. Everyone went one by one till it was my turn. Everyone was leaving the control center before me. They said they did not know anything. When I arrived inside the office, I was informed that I was there because I was the unit rep. They asked what happened and asked if this was over. I informed the inspector that I was sleeping when all went down. So I did not know what events transpired. I told him by my understanding, someone had had their property stolen and that everything was over and back to normal. He tried to get more information from me, but I kept with my story. He sent me back to the unit. When I spoke to Newell, he told me they threatened to ride him out. If he did not stay out of trouble. I told him not to worry. It was time to go get our praise over the fight. When we arrived back at our unit, everyone had a lot of cheers. For us, it felt good to feel respected. Even though we did not get written up, which we should have, I still felt good. If anything, if one wanted to rob me again, next time, they would think twice. It was not the fact that we fought and gotten away, it was more about we stood up for ourselves, period. JB, Black's bunkie, pulled me to the side and told me that they were not coming back. He also told me that during the fight, his TV cord got ripped from the back of his TV. He needed a whole new TV. I told him not to worry about it. Being on the warden's form had its benefits; I would have the inmate benefit fund pay for it. Due to the fact I liked JB until this happened, I would take turns watching my TV with him. I still read a lot for the most part. It would not brother me to not watch TV. Later that night, while speaking with Roman and Bell, Roman apologized to me for the role that he had played in the robbery. He told me that he would pay back what he could even though I told him that was not called for. Instead, truthfully, I did not want to close the door on still getting him back. I let this go for now. Bell and JB both talked with me. They were worried that this was not over. It was what it was—done was done. He was worried that I wanted the seventy-five dollars back. I told him to keep what he had that he did not have to worry about me doing anything else. I expressed to them that where I was from, when two men have a difference and they fight, regardless of the outcome, they hug, make up, and move on, and that's what we did. Boy, was his face messed up. I walked a few laps around the yard with JB. I knew him from around the unit and all but not on a personal level. I knew that from fighting the guys that robbed me, we would get a lot more friends.

JB started telling me about his case. Also, how long he had been in prison. He started summing up his prison story. He told me he was in prison for killing two people in self-defense. JB was old school, but as we talked, I found high respect for him and his struggle. After about a week of inmates giving us food, inmates that we never talked to before were talking to us.

During this time, Newell was told to pack up. He was riding out to a different prison. I was sick; we had become real cool. I learned from doing time that random ride outs were a part of doing time. Besides, we all knew that the fight had something to do with this. A few days later, Newell's mom wrote me a letter to inform me that Newell was sent to one of the fairest prisons in Michigan, up north. She also sent me half of the seventy-five dollars that was taken from us. I needed it—the little food that I had in my footlocker I had split with Newell before he left so that he would have something to eat. I stopped running the store since the fight. But I needed to get things back started again.

Buzz, my cubby, seemed very impressed with the way that I handled myself in the fight. One night, we talked and he promised that with my thirty-five dollars, he would invest one hundred dollars into running a store. That was all I needed. Buzz had real money, with his help, the sky was the limit. Soon thereafter, things did get back to normal. I would be lying if I said that I did not have a big head from all that had transpired. With Newell gone, I found myself alone again. I had Louis, Freddy, and Sagnasty, among others that I could talk to. However, my friendship with all of them was different from what I needed and was looking for.

One day in the unit, East Side came to talk to me and was talking about a new inmate that rode in not too long ago. He felt he was kind of funny. I asked him, "Funny how?" What was he trying to say?

He told me, "Funny as in homosexual." He said he had mentioned this to me because throughout my time at Bethany Creek, he assumed I was bisexual. I informed him I was not like that. I just had a bad experience at Bethany Creek. By the look on his face, I sensed he believed I was lying. I let this go and moved on. Later, I thought to myself East Side did not tell me who the guy was. I found myself asking why I even cared.

Another block rep's election came and went again. I had won another seat on the board. the difference this time I was voted to become the board chairman which was very cool. Everything would have to go through me. My first order of business was to get JB's money to get him a TV from the prisoners' fund within my second term. I had built a good relationship with the warden, Nick, after a meeting with him. While talking to me, he told me when I was ready, he would ride me out to a close-to-home prison to start getting visits to see my family. Truth of the matter was that I should have taken him up on this offer. But I asked him if the offer would still stand at the end of this block rep term. He said yes. I had stopped talking to everyone from back home. I could not recall the last time I had heard from Crissy. Besides, I still had a lot of time left, since I had let the streets go. I lived my life in prison and left everyone alone in the streets. It seemed as time was passing fast. I found myself not nearly as depressed as I used to be when Crissy was around.

Speaking of Crissy, Louis still gave me his newspapers after he read them. Days later after I won the election while reading the paper, I was reading an article about a lady stealing money from her niece and nephew. I looked at the picture that was in the paper of the lady, and I knew I recognized her. I had seen her before; her last name was Friday, Crissy's aunt. The newspaper did not say Crissy or her brother's name. But I knew it was them. It said Crissy's mother had died and left Crissy her brother an inheritance, and the lady spent the money. The victims had pressed charges and were living out of the state. This was how I found my son had not been in living in Michigan. I was pissed. Just when I thought that I got away from this woman, she came back into my life. As bad as I wanted to not dwell on the ordeal, I also knew that I couldn't let it get the best of me. It had been years since the last time I had spoken with Crissy. So why did it matter now? That's when it dawned on me. When we had our last fight for her not coming to visits when she had promised to, she was coming to see me face to face to let me know that she was leaving the state. I felt like shit but understood. I had time to do, so I could not let this keep me down.

Later that day, I saw Roy for the first time. When I saw him, I realized that he was the inmate that East Side had talked about. He stood about the same height as me, hair also on his shoulders, and had big blue eyes. He did not look boyish in any manner. There was something also feminine about him. As crazy as this sounds, I kinda did a double-take when I saw him. I think he saw that I played it off by asking him if he needed any block rep forms. He said no and walked away. I realized that he looked familiar. I had seen him around before. I had just had so much going on that I did not pay any mind. I remember Dave who was in my cubb; he would chase this inmate around. I thought to myself as block rep, I would have a talk with him. This would not be harmful to me in the eyes of others. I would just have to pick the right time to catch him alone.

A few days later, when we received store goods, my cubby Buzz basically gave me his one-hundred-dollar store bag to invest into our store. Of course, we had to pay a few bills here and there, but it was not much. Now I could work. We were getting down to where we could only purchase one or two pouches at a time. Limits on how much we could order were in place to wing us down from nicotine. The price value was also going up at this point. One could get five roll-ups for a soap. Now they were like two dollars a pop. Living off state pay at about ten dollars a month—that cut a lot for most. Things were not bad yet with stealing and fighting for tobacco. I and everyone knew this was only going to be a matter of time. I still hung out with Old School and went to school every day. Off times, we still smoked weed and drank spud juice together. He still used heroin a lot and tried to get me to use it. But that was not my drug of choice. For the most part, I left it alone. A good thing was at this time, we were almost done with school. We had inquired about the test answers, so we were flying through the test. There was a problem with hands-on things that we had to do. We eventually found an inmate to do our work for us. Things were going well.

Back in the unit, everything with Buzz was going well. He would, for the most part, go to the store and give me his whole store bag. Together we started to smoke up and drink more than we were bringing in. So Buzz started having his sister send me between $150 to $200 between store periods. I owned restitution for court cost, so they would take anything from $50 to $75 out of the money that Buzz was sending me. Buzz did not care, I did not either; that was money being paid off. One day, I would eventually have to pay this debt. But if Buzz wanted to help, more power to him.

CHAPTER SEVENTEEN

Lost

A while after on a rainy day, after coming back from the chow line, I saw Roy walking alone. We were authorized to go to the big yard from the chow line. On different occasions, I would try to make conversation with Roy, only to find people around that made me feel very uncomfortable. So for the most part, we would never talk when I got to the big yard and caught up with him. I asked if he wanted company; he said he did not mind. I felt as if something was bothering him. Anybody else, I probably would have walked away and gave them their alone time. I also knew if not at all, I would probably not get another chance to speak with him again. Alone in the rain we walked and talked; I did most of the talking. After about five or six laps, I was soaking wet, so I left the yard. I found out that Roy did play chess and had his own board. He promised that one of these days, he would find some time to play. While walking off I thought to myself how cool I thought Roy was. I was older then him; however, we liked the same music. A few of our friends around the prison were mutual. There was something about Roy that I felt comfortable with. I felt as if I could talk to him about anything. The crazy thing was that I didn't even really know him. Prison was not the place where one just walks up to people. Prisoners use your confessions or innermost secrets against you. I learned that a long time ago.

My bunkie and I were still closer than ever. He was still studying to be a counselor. Any time he had the opportunity, he would
practice what he was learning on me. I listened and I believed—that's
why he worked on me so much. Anybody else would have probably
told him to get lost. In truth, I liked the things he talked about. In
a lot of ways, he did make me start answering some real questions
about myself. He would get really deep. The only thing that I did not
care for was the fact that I would never really be able to give some
of my input. So I would listen. It was that day that he told me that
he was going home soon. We both did our own thing. For the most
part, we never really got into each other's way or business. But it was
going to suck to watch him go. Sometimes he overdid our conversations. But I did like to listen most of the time. I would like to believe
that in spite of doing all this time in prison and a little trouble as a
juvenile that I was not a bad person. I had just made some bad decisions in my life. My bunkie was starting to make me believe it.

That same day, I got my first letter from Newell. It was good
to finally hear from him. He told me about how they had sent him
all the way to a prison in the upper peninsula. He was in a different
time zone. He expressed how he really did not care he would be
going home soon. He also informed me he had gotten a good job.
He ended his letter with a promise that after he got home, he would
look out for me and would walk the rest of my time down with
me. I thought that was very nice. I took the letter to Freddy. Newell
wanted me to tell him that he said hi. I liked Freddy; we were cool
as hell. I started to notice that he was doing a lot of pills. Pills were
not my thing, but I agreed to do some with him. We got Sag Nasty
and Flint together and tried to get them to join us. They said they
would not. We were all cool—it just was not what they got into,
which I respected, and keep it moving with Pun, learning about all
the money I was bringing in with him, Buzz, and a few more homeboys who started giving me door calls all of a sudden and wanting to
hang out. I was a jokester, so I bragged about how good I was doing.
I smoked weed with them and paid for it to kind of throw my weight
around. Deep down inside, the crazy thing was I did not care for
them. I also realized they did not give a shit about me. When other

inmates where we were from saw me grouped up with them, they did not hang out with us. They knew of Pun from back home and proceeded to tell me stories about him. I was informed he was a bad ass and a lot of people were scared of him from the things he used to be into back in the day. I would just watch my back around him. For the most part, Buzz was taking care of me. I felt that as long as I put it out, it would keep coming back in with interest. Then he would keep doing business with me. Buzz was definitely more of a follower than a leader. I knew I needed to keep my investment close so no one would be able to step on my toes. I realized that others knew how good we were doing and would try to pull Buzz away. So I started going to the chow, every meal with him.

Most prisons in Michigan have white and black segregated sides to eat chow. All the blacks sat on one side, while all the whites sat on the other side. Most of the white people liked me, so it was not a problem for me to sit on the white side. That was the first time that I had seen Val; he was what we called he/she in prison. A man in body; everything else was all girly. Val; he had another he/she with him. Val was not the first he/she that I had seen over the years doing time. Honestly speaking, there was something about Val that I liked. So from time to time, I would catch eye contact with Val. I thought to myself that I would never talk with him but would eat on that side for now on to see him. I found time and asked Roy if he wanted to play chess with me. He agreed, I found he really sucked, to keep him interested, I would let him win so that he would keep playing. He told me that he liked my hair and asked if I could do his. I knew that his hair was too straight but I would try nonetheless.

Nard came to the window while we were playing chess. He looked at me then Roy and gave me a mischievous look, as if I were up to no good. I did not pay this any mind though. Louis entered the dayroom. I'm guessing Nard went and got him. They were together at the window when I noticed Louis also gave me that weird look as if I were up to something again. I paid this no mind and kept it moving. Roy and I started hanging out a lot. One of the inmates from around the unit started calling him Surfer boy, and it stuck because of his hair. It wasn't long before we were taking pills and smoking weed all the time. Besides, I already knew about Roy from East Side. Other people from the yard started informing me that he liked boys and girls. They began asking me what my business was with him. I just made up stories at the time to keep the homeboys off my back. I had never asked Roy what he had done in his personal time. I liked Roy and did not want to mess up our friendship. So I would be lying to say that I was not curious to know the truth. I asked him one day. I believe at first, it threw him off. At first, he did not respond to yes or no; he just sat there. Then finally, after a while, he said that he was not. It was in his response how I then knew the truth. He did like boys. I felt that I would let him open up about it to me in his own time.

By now, I pretty much stopped working out altogether. I just was not into it, between running my store, smoking weed, taking pills, and just not being able to find the time. One evening, while talking with Louis and Nard, I found out that Nard was the supplier of weed. He was the man, my workout partner, and I did not know this. Of course, he made me swear to secrecy, as long as we broke bread. I was going to not say anything. So I started getting good deals for Buzz and me. We were smoking weed damn near every day. That was around the first time I was called to the control center to take my first drug test. When I was told to go to the control center during count time, I already knew what time it was. When I got there, the CO that was taking the urine cup would talk with me, whispering every time the other CO left the room. He was asking me about an inmate from next door during the time I was over there. The inmate that he described, I knew as G. He was my Mexican homeboy from Pine River and MTU. I told the CO his family was my homeboy. After that, I felt that I could trust the CO, so I took a chance and peed in a cup. I was going to get a substance abuse Ticket anyway. So I asked him if opiates could be found in a urine test. He proceeded asking me why. I informed him that three days ago, I had taken Vicodin. He told me not to worry about it. I did my business and left. I never got a ticket.

A few days later, I took some pills called Tagertall; we just called them tags. Tagertall was keeping us up for days at a time. Roy and

I saved up for the late-night TV room; only five people could go in there, so we had quite a time. Since we were so high, I thought that we were going into the dayroom to laugh and have a good time. Roy surprised me and handed me a letter saying read by myself and throw it away when I was done after understanding what was going on and made my way to my cube to read the letter. Upon opening the folder results from a doctor stating Roy was clean, along with his letter he expressed how much he liked me and wanted me to come meet him in the shower first thing in the morning I had found myself shocked and speechless.

The next morning, I went to the bathroom early, and just like he said he would be, Roy was in the shower. I proceeded back to my room, put my shower things together, and walked to the bathroom. When I was certain the coast was clear, I went in there with him. I have no excuses for what I did. I knew I had made a conscience decision. I would have to live with it for the rest of my life.

I started to be known as the Book Man around the time that Vaga rode in from next door (Pine River). The Book Man meant that you were into freak books, nasty books like pornography, etc. For the most part, not all but a lot of the freak books were going through my hands, so if you wanted to look at a book you came to see me. When Vaga rode in—him being Mexican, they took care of their own—he started hanging out with Polo. I remembered Vaga from next door, we really did not talk. I did talk with Polo because a lot of books passed through his hands as well.

On the side, I still did my block rep duties and always talked with Ms. Jacks, our unit Arus. A few times, I was even sure that she was checking me out when we were alone in her office. I never said anything out of the way because I did not want to take her kindness for a weakness. Al, the old men were still around, like the old man that had that crazy sex case. One day, me being block rep and all, he asked me to help him fill out some paperwork to order some clothes from a vendor. While helping him, jokingly, I asked him to order me something. He said that if I walked and talked with him time to time, he would get me whatever I wanted. For starters, just to call his bluff, I had him order some socks, books, shirts, and boxers. I also had him put in a store list for fifty dollars just to see if he was for real. He got everything. The problem was that lately, I had been getting a lot of my homeboys or inmates that I kicked it with asking me questions about Roy, everyone thinking him to be homosexual. If I started openly walking around with Al, him being openly homosexual, I would never hear the end of it. Let's face it, though—no one from home was looking out for me. My school pay was only about five to seven dollars a month. I did have the store thing going with Buzz and was doing well, might I add. I guess I wanted more. So when no one was around, I started walking with Al. Even though he was freaky and had that messed-up case, he was not that bad. For the most part, he just wanted me to walk and listen to him, and I did. I was surprised that he never asked me to do something that I was not going to do. He just wanted me to listen. For what he was paying, I was all ears.

Not long after, my bunkie was told to pack his things; he was riding out. We talked that whole evening. He told me he would check in on me from time to time. I believed him. Brock was my bunkie and we got along well. I don't believe that he ever told me anything wrong. The truth of the matter was that he was positively shaping me for the world. I knew I would never forget Brock. The next morning, I walked him to the control center to his ride out.

As he was leaving, my new bunkie came in. His blues looked like hand-me-downs as if he had been possibly living out of a truck outside. When we arrived at the unit, he said his name was Moon but people preferred to call him Wolfman. He said that he had done documentaries and had been on CNN about his raising and relationships with wolves. We opened conversation; we talked. I told him most of the rules to watch out for. That was it for the most part. He informed me he would be in the presence of the board soon. He expected to be leaving soon. So I walked to the office and asked for the bottom bunk. I was told to come back after he left to get the bunk. At this time, we were at the last store where we could order cigarettes. Prior to this, we were given a date when the cigarettes had to stop being sold. The other units felt it was unfair because A and B units were the first to get the store. Since the date was in the next few days, other units would not be able to get smokes. We went to the wardens' form to fight this issue, to get the other units one more store for tobacco, and the warden agreed. A lot of inmates were very happy. Again, no one believed that they were going to let cigarettes get taken out of the system. COs and inmates alike, everyone was counting on lifers in the higher levels to start riots so that they would stop the process of our cigarettes getting taken. So after, the warden gave every unit one last store for tobacco. We had one month till inmates were to have all tobacco products gone. Pretty much, for the most part, after three to five days, everyone's tobacco was almost gone. It was about to get tight. It was no secret that the homeboy Gamble had at least six to ten pouches left. Giving him the low end and saying that he only had four pouches, he was still looking at sixteen dollars. You could buy a pouch for two dollars out of the store. But selling them in singles rolled up, you could easily make something like $100. I liked Gamble, but everyone knew that he was a target. Others that were holding in other units were starting to get hit. Shortly after, as the days went by, I would hear guys getting hit and robbed for matches, rolling papers, cans of tobacco, and pouches. Where homeboy Gamble went wrong was he got greedy. I only make that observation from the outside looking in. It was widely known that he had at least seven lockers full of food from selling tobacco and running a store. Instead of cutting his homeboys in, he would go to outsiders to sell the tobacco for him. This really pissed Louis off. I was not really mad or upset about it. If I wanted to have the things he did, I could and would have easily saved my tobacco pouches. It was his time to grind. In fact, it was good to see him doing well. Anytime I ever needed anything, he would gave it to me with a promise to just give it back. Louis always talked about strong-arming him, but I never paid him any mind. For the most part, I would just laugh with him.

One night, Louis walked down to the cubb to ask him for a cigarette. Gamble told him to pay for it. Louis snapped, took all the cigarettes—fifty to eighty cigarettes—and walked up the hallway, passing them out to anyone with their hand out. It did not hit me that these rollups could be Gamble's. I just had my hand out like so many inmates. After the cigarettes were all gone, I saw Gamble and

Louis having words. I put two and two together: Louis had taken them. I walked to Gamble to return the few that I had. He was so sick that he did not want them. He did not want anything to do with Louis on the fighting tip. After he said what he wanted to say, he walked down to his cubb. As bad as it was, what Louis did to Gamble, everyone knew he was really upset and hurt. The question was how was he going to retaliate. If he did not fight, others would think he was soft and take his things. They would know then that he would not stand up for himself. As bad as this may sound, it was the truth. People were ready to eat. If Gamble did not tell the COs or fight, his little time that he had left was going to be a hard time.

CHAPTER EIGHTEEN

Showtime

One night, I got with Polo, and we got a book (pornography). This one was special; the inmates that rented them from me would pay top dollars to see this. An inmate by the name of Double R came around to my cubb to see if I had any books. His timing could not have been worse; I told him that I had one at the end of my bunk. Once he had it in his hand, from the look in his eye, I then knew that I would be able to kill his pocket. One must understand most of these inmates are rapists or child molesters, so most of their will-power was out of control.

Double R asked me if he could take the book. I told him, "Not now, come back later." He asked me whose it was. I told him Polo's. I did not think that he would, but he went and asked Polo. Polo told him to take his time with it. Since I was showing everyone, Double R came back and told me what Polo said. I was watching a show that I did not want to miss. So I was not trying to argue. I told Double R not to take the book from my cubb. He did anyway. In my eyes, that was considered stealing. Or that's how I took it. I wanted to fight. Double R was JB's right-hand man. Since my last fight, JB and I got cool as hell, since the time when Newell broke his TV and I let him watch mine. Every day that I did not have it, he did. Plus we started breaking bread, going to beat Double R's ass. This would be disrespectful without talking to JB. So I walked across the hall to see what he thought about it. It threw me off, after telling JB what happened and what I wanted to do. He gave me the go-ahead to beat Double R up. Even with the go-ahead, I still felt wrong for fighting him. But I could easily be persuaded even though Double R was JB's homeboy. JB said Double R was in need to get put into his place. I walked around to Double R's cubb, which was in the front hallway. On the way there, Freddy saw me and asked what was wrong with me. He told me that the last time he had seen that look in my face, Newell and I had gotten into that big fight. I told him quickly what happened with Double R, that I was walking around to check him. Freddy told me to be careful.

When I got around to where Double R locked at, he was on his bed watching TV. Normally, one should not walk into others' cubbs. But I was so mad I did not care whom I made mad. The plan was to go to him talking trash in hopes he would say something—I mean anything—then I was going to fight him. When I walked in totally talking, he did not say a word; he knew better.

After walking out of his cell, I still felt the dissatisfaction. I wanted action and went looking for it. The next person on the list that I was mad at was Polo. I walked into the dayroom. He and a few of his homeboys were in there. The only one that might interfere that I thought of was Vaga. I did not believe he would get into our fight if it did come down to it. Polo was at the toaster as soon as I entered the room. I started talking trash to him, or better yet, I was expressing myself to him. With the things that I was saying to him in an angry way, at one time during our heated conversation, I jumped at him as if I was going to sucker-punch him. He saw it and kind of backed up a little. I can't say how I allowed myself to get this mad. But I made it seen as if I was going to hit him again. He reacted faster; he sucker-punched me in the face. Truthfully, that's what I was waiting for. With the officers' station able to see us, we were kind of pushing our luck, fighting like that. Nonetheless, it was on. We were kind of fighting our way toward the back of the dayroom, where the emergency exit was. Polo was bigger than me. I was pushing him back with punches. I give him credit; he was holding his ground.

What changed the fight was that I started getting the better of Polo. I would like to believe that Vaga's intentions were good from what he did next, but it did not seem that way. He tried to break up the fight, but he grabbed me from the back. What he should have done was grab Polo from the back, them being homeboys and all, or he should have come in the middle between us when Vaga had me in his arms. Polo was getting hit after hit in. I would go as far as to say that Vaga popped one or two himself. This is not what had me mad. I was mad because while these two were jumping me, none of my brothers did anything to help me. I had to think quickly, the funny thing was that I had never been jumped before. My crazy ass did always wish for the experience of it. I hit Vaga with an elbow. This knocked him back and gave me the window that I needed. I needed to do something to Polo. I hit him so hard it knocked him straight off his feet out of the emergency room exit door. Now mind you, this was third shift. For an inmate to be outside for any reason without an escort was an attempted escape, no questions asked. I stood there looking down at him and realized that Vaga was still there. I turned around while the door was sounding off loudly—*beep, beep, beep*. Vaga stood there. I sucker-punched him in the eye. I told him, "Bitch, don't ever put your hands on me." He yelled back, and it was on; I knew that it was. So while leaving the dayroom on my way to put on my shoes, Louis stopped me and asked what happened. I told him Polo and Vaga had jumped me while running to my room. I heard him trying to confirm if what I said was true. I had to get my shoes. I knew that this was not over.

When I got to my cubb, my bunkie was watching my TV. He saw how hard I was breathing and asked me what was wrong. While putting my shoes on, I told him I had been jumped. As I looked up, Vaga was standing in my cubb doorway. I walked to the door just as Vaga was tying his boot. I was getting prepared for round two, the whole time keeping my eyes on Vaga. From the corner of my eyes, I could see the hallway as well as over the wall that was between the high side hallway and low side hallway. People were everywhere. I had a show to put on. Vaga was a lot bigger than I was. I was confident that I would be stronger and faster going into this fight. I had a great eye for sizing people up but have to admit I was wrong about Vaga. He was stronger and faster than I thought.

We squared off, and I hit him first. I did not want to take any chances with him. He was much bigger than me. I loved to fight, but I felt I was even better at wrestling. So I took him to the ground with a slam. I tried to regain control by getting on top in order to deliver a bunch of punches to his face. That's when I realized how strong and fast he was. It was hard to overpower him. Since he had good ground defense himself, it was hard to punch him in the face. I would have liked to. Besides, at this point, I was getting tired. Truthfully, I don't know how I lasted that long. Louis pulled me off the top of him. In my mind, I was thanking God. The emergency exit was still sounding off. The COs still had not come out of the office. Vaga got up, talking trash about how much of a gangster he was. I yelled that gangsters get their ass beat too; the back hallway laughed. Vaga still went on talking. Louis looked at me and told me to hold his glasses. I knew there was about to be trouble. This is when everyone came from nowhere. Most of the Muskegon homeboys came out. I saw a few of them hitting Vaga. Polo made his way to the back hallway. He was pleading for us to stop. Louis was working on Vega. He punched him out the back hallway emergency exit. So now you had two doors beeping loudly. Again, Cos was nowhere to be found. The only way for the alarm to be turned off was for them to reset it with keys. Before Vaga could get back into the door, Louis shut it. Other inmates pleaded for Louis to open the door to let him back in. We all knew to get caught out there was an escape charge. Louis would not allow it, and I was not mad at him. For about five minutes or so, things kind of cooled down. As soon as Vaga came down the hallway still talking like a gangster, Louis was right behind him. It was back on again. This time, Polo was with him. I swung and missed. Polo would have been on my ass if it would not have been for my homeboy, Big Boy from Skeetown. When I got off the ground, I looked up just in time to see Louis. He had lifted Vaga up over his head to slam him. When Vaga hit the ground, the whole back hall was like, "Ouch."

After he hit the ground, Louis hit him in the face. I could tell that he was knocked out. One of my cubbies said, "Jerry, go get Louis before he kills him."

I grabbed his arms and said, "Louis, that's enough."

When Vega got up off the ground this time, he did not say a word. It was now getting close to count time. The incident calmed down, and everyone got to their bunks. The COs doing the round said that the dayroom and back hallway emergency exit door was opened. He closed them and finished his rounds. I thought to myself, *That whole time that we fought, the COs did not do a round.* Normally, the COs do rounds every half hour. We were lucky. I remember thinking to myself, was it over or not?

Vaga's face was messed up really bad. I thought about locking in the bunk facing the hallway—would he stick me while I was sleeping? An inmate from the front side called me in the closed day oom to talk with Polo. I went to see what he had to say. He apologized and said things should not have gone that far. He was right; we agreed it was over. Louis was not easily convinced to let things go. But I did convince him. I still was going to watch my back and was not going to sleep well at all that night.

The next day, Monday morning, it did not take long for snitches and rats to send a kite to tell the counselor Ms. Jacks, and the COs what happened last night. Everything seemed as if it was going to go smoothly until an inmate that was all right with me said he was at the board reading block rep material when he heard Polo, Vaga, and other Mexican inmates talking about getting me when I least expected it. When he told me, I was very upset because Louis wanted to make him lock up but I talked him out of it. So I, Louis, and a few more other homeboys went into the dayroom to see if they wanted more, and if we felt they did, we would make them lock up. The leader of the Mexicans, I was cool with. We called him Mexico, he gave me his word that things should have never gone that far. He told me it was over, and I believed him.

Shortly after, Arus Jacks called us in her office one by one. Vega went first. I truthfully thought that he was telling. His face was all messed up. He came out and nothing happened. I knew that he did not tell. She called Polo into her office next. Nothing happened when he came out too. Then she called me in. First thing she said was, "Is it over?" I said that I did not know what she was talking about. She turned and looked at me from the computer and said, "Mr. Ready, is it over." She said that she did not know everything, just what other inmates wrote in kites to her. She knew that there were others involved; she just did not know who. She had made up her mind that someone was going to get moved from the unit. It was just a matter of whom? I sure the hell did not want to move, so I told her that if there was going to be any more trouble, it would be from Vaga. She told me to say no more.

Later that day, Vaga was told to move to a different unit. Not too long after, Old School and I got to a point that if we wanted to, we could be done with school. We both just wanted to do what was necessary to get our trade certificate. Old School and I both accomplished getting our certificate. I was beginning to get to know my bunkie, Moon, a lot better. Boy, was he nasty. He was good people. I did not smell him, nothing like that. He would eat very old food. He would have old food in his bed while sleeping. I just thought it was funny. Buzz did not like him. When Moon would leave, Buzz would do stuff to his bunk. I had to tell Buzz to stop. He was getting carried away. A good quality about Moon was his artistic skills. He could draw very well. I started having people draw in my journal, so I wrote in them. It would look cool. So Moon drew for me. Everything was still, going strong for me on the warden form. Nick the warden, after every meeting, would ask me if I was ready to have him put me on the transfer closer to home. I always said I need a little more time. At worst, I would take the transfer at the end of my term. With all the fights that I had been in, I was gaining a lot of respect in prison. For a small guy, I was getting a lot of attention from a lot of different people. I was engaging in things that most others would have gotten a lot of open criticism for.

Most thought me and Roy were having a relationship. I still was sitting on the white side of the chow hall just to see Val. Roy started acting funny all of a sudden. He was getting close to home. He wanted to back off and stop messing around. We did, and I was very upset about it. I had been doing time for years at this time. I read books on how to manipulate people. Roy, even though he was young, was far from dumb. I needed to find a way in. When I did, I would strike. It was not long before I found his soft spot. I knew I would be able to use it against him, and I did.

One day, while on the big yard with one of the homeboys, a young inmate by the name of Leonard started talking with me and showing me a lot of attention. This was not normal to me. Leonard was not homosexual as far as I knew. The only thing he and I had in common was I knew how to do front and back flips. He was trying to learn before he went home. While Leonard and I were talking, Roy just so happened to be walking him around the track. I saw the look on his face. I knew that he and Leonard were cool from the look on his face, how he looked at Leonard and the way he was acting toward me. I put two and two together that he liked Leonard a lot. I talked with Leonard. I told him that we would start to walk the yard. I would teach him how to backflip. Just like I thought, Roy loved that boy. Leonard was not homosexual—or at least that is what he wrote in the letter he gave me. Roy was calling me scandalous, saying that I was doing stuff with Leonard, when that was so far from the truth. I believed he believed that because of the way our relationship with each other was. Yet at the same time, Leonard was the only leverage that I had on Roy. I was going to use this leverage that I had on Roy. I was going to use his insecurity with Leonard and me to my advantage. So I did not deny his accusations about Leonard and me, which drove Roy crazy. I would walk and talk with Leonard alone. I would make sure it was in places where Roy would see us. I would lead Leonard into it. I would have him bring up conversation about Roy and his sexuality. Leonard knew that Roy liked him. He also told me about how people told him to watch out for me. He did not think that I was like that, so we stayed cool. Leonard continued to give me door calls, and I continued to teach him how to flip and spend time with him just to get under Roy's skin and get him back in the order of things. I can say that it was working Roy was begging for me to take him back to the point that he would do anything.

I was enjoying the power I had over him. I planned to rub it in just a little bit more so I could enjoy it. The whole time, I had been informing Roy that Leonard and I had nothing going, and we didn't to make things worse, I wrote a letter in nasty handwriting that did not look like mine. Roy knew my handwriting, so I wrote the letter to myself as if Leonard wrote it to me, expressing his deep love for me and how he could not live without me. I threw more in the letter; his love for me was the basis of the letter. So I kept it simple. I knew that Roy would be running around to my cubb sometime real soon. I placed the letter on my bunk and waited for him to come. Shortly after, he did just as I imagined. He reached over my body and got the letter. I had to act and make it seem as if it was important, something that he was not supposed to have. I begged him to give it back. I made facial expressions of concern and hurt. He knew that he had something that he thought was from Leonard. We started fighting each other for the letter. We were doing everything short of punching each other in the face. My cubbies didn't like it, but I did not care. I let things go on like that for about five minutes. Then I let Roy go; he walked out with the letter. I knew that after Roy read this letter, no matter what I said, there was no going back.

When Roy came back around, I could see the hurt in his face. But he was taking it well. Roy felt that I had the power to influence Leonard to be with him. Even though I knew I did not, I played along. Roy said that if I made Leonard his, then he would be mine. So I played the game, all the while having my way with Roy while the getting was good. I knew that eventually Roy would catch on.

Not long thereafter, my bunkie Moon rode out, and I was moved to the bottom bunk. I did not want the top bunk any longer. On Saturday nights, we would sometimes get *Girls Gone Wild*, the UFC fights, or PPV boxing. On those days, I would easily have fifteen inmates around my TV, and I did not like that. The bottom bunk was a little more private. My homeboy Raw Raw that had locked in a different unit now was pretty much walking around with a boy. To my understanding, they were together. I did not think it was bad what he was doing, but others did. It was one thing to do it in a private place but in the open, not caring, was a whole thing in itself. Truthfully, inside, I liked Raw Raw all the more for not giving a damn what people thought of him. I was not strong enough to face that about myself just yet. I was getting better. So one day, while at chow for like two days, Val did not show up to chow, I went to Raw Raw's unit, gave him a door call, and asked him about Val. He gave me some insightful information. I told him to tell Val he did not have to come to chow. Then we could not play our game, which was catching eye contact while we ate. When Raw Raw first came out, he said Val did not know whom I was talking about. But eventually Val came around that he was talking about me. I said okay days later, which was the first time that I said anything to Val. We were both coming out of the chow hall. I was with Buzz; Val was with a different he/she. I needed a light for a rollup. I asked them for one. Val reached to give me the matches. While grabbing the match, I rubbed his hand. From then, it was on.

Cigarettes were becoming scarce. I got lucky. One of my cubbies, Cookie, had a lot of cigarettes left still, we made a deal that if I sold his for him, he would give me tobacco. I did; for that short time, I was the man. I was one of the only people in the little world that had tobacco. It was crazy fun. I started to notice that a few of the homeboys were talking about taking Gamble's stuff. No one knew how to do it. So I took the initiative and knew who was the man for the job, but first, I had to ask if everyone was all right with it. So I talked to Louis and Flint since they were in the cubb. He was the ringleader and so was Sagnasty. I got them all together and said that we should have East Side break the lock. I guess that seemed to be the hardest part for everyone. It seemed that they did not want to let him in.

The next day, before anything could happen, I decided to play devil's advocate. On the day of the robbery, I went to one of Gamble's closest inmate friends that he was always with and whom I trusted and told him to tell Gamble that he was going to be hit so to watch himself. If someone like Louis or Flint found out that I was working both sides, it could have been a lot of trouble for me, but I knew that Gamble would look out for me and that he also would point me out to be one of the good guys that had his back. I knew that no matter how long it took, they were going to get Gamble; it was just a matter of time.

Gamble took well the information that I told him or relayed to him. Later, he sent me a bag of food down. I was getting the best of both worlds. I found out that as soon as the opportunity presented itself, Flint that locked in the cubb with Gamble was going to pick his lock. It did not take long for the opportunity to come; it was later that day. While trying to pop the lock, Flint could not do it. Gamble had some kind of device that made things very hard for Flint to open the lock. While I and others watched out, we sent Flint to try again, and it worked. Since no one knew where Gamble had hidden the tobacco, they took everything that they could get their hands on in the short amount of time that they had. Flint ran down the hallway with a sheet filled with food, and though it on my bunk, I was very upset. Even though I was watching out, I did not want anything that could be traced back to me. I quickly removed the bag from my bed and hid it behind the locker. I really wanted to check and see if the tobacco was hidden in the food. After checking and going through every bit, I could not find anything. Flint came down the hallway and informed me that East Side had jumped over the wall while Flint was in the act of popping the lock. It was he (East Side) who had gotten the locker open, and it was he that had the tobacco. There were three pouches even though there were a lot of us that was into the plot. Three pouches was more than enough money to go around. Rounding it off, it was about twelve hundred dollar's easy. How we did this was, Louis split his with Sagnasty. Since East Side popped the lock, he got to keep his to himself. I split my portion with Flint. On top of that, Flint and I got to keep and split the bag of food. Gamble came off the yard. He was very upset; he even told the Cos, but they did nothing.

After selling my tobacco, I had easily made two hundred dollars. After, things got back to what I would call normal. One day on the yard, Raw Raw introduced me to Val. First, I was avoiding this at all costs. I did not want people to talk about me behind my back. It was one thing to hang with Roy. People assumed him to be bisexual, but it was not confirmed. It was not guessing at that point. I did tell one or two people that I trusted Roy to be around. Val was a whole different story; he was girly and very flamboyant. Since it was cold outside and there were not a lot of people out, I went out to meet him. We walked and got to know each other better. More than anything, I was interested in his story. I wanted to know how he came about the way that he was. During chow line, we started walking together. Again, in normal cases where others would get talked about or openly criticized, I got nothing. If things were said about me, it was behind my back. What I did not know would not hurt me. So I did what I did.

One day while on the yard with Pun and a few of the homeboys, they did ask me questions about Val and why I talked to him. So I used my store as an excuse. That one always worked. A few of them did not let it go so easily; they kept at the questioning. I noticed that Pun always took up for me. Or when he and I were alone, he spoke in kind favor toward the other homeboys. Not really understanding, I got the feelings that Pun's feelings were a lot deeper than he was willing to tell me about, so I let it go at that.

Later one day, while out on yard, I was on crew duty with Pun and a few of the homeboys. Val was walking the yard. I saw how Val looked at Pun and Pun looked at Val in return. Something was funny about it, so I thought I would talk with Val about this at dinner. When everyone left the table, I asked Val what he thought about Pun. At first, he was holding back, but when he realized I was not going to let up, he told me they had done time before at a different prison and that they were sexually active with each other. Val asked me not to say anything. Truthfully, a lot of things did not shock me at this point of doing time. But that did—I would have never guessed. Val made me promise that I would not say anything. I gave my word.

Two days later, Val was caught having sex with an inmate in the shower by a CO. Somebody had told. This made time with Val even harder; we did not have sex or anything for that matter. This time in my life, a person would not understand unless they lived in this world or did a lot of time. They would not understand the friendship/relationship that Val and I had. Explaining this in words,

I would just say that were I was missing the friendship/love from Crissy or family. Val filled that hole. Moving on with Val, he moved to a different unit, a loss of privilege (LOP). I was never going to see him. Everyone knew that it was just a matter of time before Val was sent to a higher level. This is when we both came up with a plan to leave together. I would use the warden to send me to the same place as Val instead of close to home. After, we went over the plan that we would put in place.

One morning after we said our goodbyes, Val walked to the Control Center and refused to lock down. They did not like the idea of Val leaving that way. They kept him in the control center for like two days. This was unheard of. Most inmates that lock up that way only stay in the control center for a few hours. Roy and Al were doing pretty much anything that I wanted. Al was going to the store for me and ordering clothes and shoes. Roy was giving me all his money, still trying to get me to hook him and Leonard up.

It was about a week after Val had left that a family member rode in—Buck. While coming off the backyard talking with Roy, Buck walked up on me. I did not recognize him, so I said "Excuse me" and continued on my way.

Buck said, "Bullet, for real."

I looked at him. At first, I did not know who he was.

He said, "It's me, Buck."

My first cousin Buck and I had been pretty much inseparable from childhood. Honestly, it was good to see real family, someone that I really had love for. Yet at the same time, I knew that a lot of things that I had been doing were going to slow down. I knew that some of the things I was doing were starting to reach the street. First things first—I went over to the unit to make Buck a care package. Mostly food and hygiene. We sat and caught up with each other about things from the past that had happened since we'd been locked up. It was crazy to find out he had four kids. That was one of the bad things about leaving the streets behind, things change that I don't know about. With Buck there, he and I would not be far apart, and I was fine with that. In fact, we started kicking off things as if we'd never left after catching up on a few things. Since getting high off pills was the major thing at this time, that's what I put an order in for. We started taking pills, Roy, Freddy, Buck, and I. Since Buck had been at the prison, I started putting a little distance between Roy so that nothing would be to obvious, yet Buck never said anything to me about it. So that was cool. For the next few weeks, that is how things went. We started smoking weed, drinking spud juice, and taking pills. With Buck around, an old side of me came out: being a clown and making a fool out of myself to make people laugh. I did not mind. I would walk around like the old man that I learned to walk and dress like. Everyone would get a kick out of that.

Things with my and Buzz's store were still doing good. With putting out food for one and a half. On top of buzz going to the store for the full amount every time and giving me the whole bag. He was also sending me anywhere from one hundred and fifty to two hundred dollars at a time. It did not take long before I received a letter from the county building saying that my restitution was finally paid. That was crazy. I never said a word to Buzz, but he had paid all my restitution. That was the shit.

Days later, I was awoken by one of the unit COs. He told me to wake up; I was moving to observation cubb. This was shocking to me. I thought that if I had done something wrong, then Ms. Jacks would have said something. She would not have just moved me. I asked if Ms. Jacks was still in the office; the CO said yes. I went and knocked at her door and inquired about what the problem was. She told me she had been receiving kites saying I was being a predator, preying on weaker inmates. She would not let me see the kites or share the names of the inmates with me. But we both knew whom she was referring to. I asked why she did not just give me a warning instead of just up and moving me. She informed that she had to do what she had to do. In my mind, I felt that I had to do what I had to do as well. I was going to refuse to lock down. I did not want to be there any longer. I felt like me getting moved would be the first steps of the COs or the administration would start messing with me.

I woke Buzz up and told him to split the store. Then I went to Buck's unit and called him out. I gave him a few things like sweatpants and jacket and told him that I was leaving. Buck knew that I was ready to go. I had been talking about leaving to him all along. Buck did try to talk me out of leaving. My mind was made up at that point. I gave him a hug and said our goodbyes. When I arrived back at the unit, the COs asked me why I was out in the yard and not moving. I told them that I was, that I had been told I had till count time to have all my things moved, which gave me almost two hours. Buzz was doing a good job splitting the food up, so that was something I did not have to worry about.

Roy must have heard what was going on; he ran down to my room, asking me what was I doing. I informed him I had been asked by the COs to move to the observation cubb. He informed me he was in the process of moving to the back hall. I told him that was cool and all but I was not going back to the observation cubb; that was out of the question. I informed him I was refusing to lock down, that I did not want to be here any longer. Like Buck and Roy knew it was only a matter of time before I was going to leave. Because I had been talking about it, I assumed no one believed me. Roy proceeded to beg me not to leave. He wanted me to stay. My mind was made up to leave. I saw some of the homeboys outside, including Freddy, Pun, and Louis. When I went and talked to Buck the first time, I did not say anything. I wanted to say goodbye. So I went back outside and told them what was happening. That is when I was called off the yard over the intercom to return to my unit. One of the unit COs came out and gave me a direct order to come in and move. After saying goodbye to them, I went back into the unit and finished packing my things. I had one of my last words with one of my cubbies, Cookie. He told me, "Jerry, from the outside looking in, please only take the words that I tell you as constructive criticism," because he would never tell another grown man what to do.

I stopped and listened. He informed me that the Jerry that had first arrived and the cubb and the Jerry now were two different people. He told me I was a leader and for the last few months, I was doing nothing but following. From the outside looking in, he said he watched me and things which were in my power of control become out of control. "No matter what happens from now on, you still have time to do, so you will overcome whatever happens again." I thought to myself that he was right.

Buzz and Cookie told me that they would watch my property till the COs came to pick it up. Refusing to lock down, I could not take it with me or I would not be allowed in the doors. I had to sneak up to the control center. I gave Roy a hug and was on my way. When I arrived at the control center, I did get into the door. If they knew that an inmate was going to lock up, they would not open the door. When I got in, they asked me what I needed. I told them I needed to see the sergeant or whoever was in charge. When a sergeant came to the window, I told him that I feared for the safety of my life, that I was refusing to lock down. He told me that a CO from the unit had called the control center and already had made them aware of what I was up to. The sergeant told the CO at the window that every hour that I was up there to write me a major ticket. I thought to myself then, this was going to be a long day. My mind was made up; there was no turning back.

It was around lunch time that Ms. Jacks came up to speak with me. Ms. Jacks and the captain called me to the back office. Everything was put on the floor. Ms. Jacks informed the captain about kites she had received from other inmates, that I was receiving money from Al, Roy, and Buzz.

I told her that all this was untrue. Well, truthfully, it was true that all of them were giving me money, just not in the way they thought. To them, I was being a predator. To me, I was hustling, making a living. The fact of the matter was that loaning or borrowing was not allowed. This was a rule, and I had been breaking it. It was not good, sound reasoning, but I felt like I didn't mess with anyone. I minded my own business, served my purpose as a block rep.

She picked on me. They came back with, "Rules are rules and you're breaking them." Ms. Jacks said that if I stopped this now, she and the captain would make all the major tickets go away. But I still would have to be in the observation cubb. I said no. We all walked out of the offices, and I sat in the control center hallway. On her way out, Ms. Jacks told me that the only place I was going from there was a level four. About five o'clock, I did not care where I went. I guess to raise my level from a one to a four, I needed my points to go up. For my points to go up, I needed major tickets. So I lay on a bench and started singing. This got a lot of people's attention. The sergeant, captain, inspector, and regular CO were yelling at me to get up. "Stop singing, this is a direct order." They told me to stop lying on the bench.

I yelled back, "I'm trying to help y'all write the ticket." After a while, they gave up asking me to stop lying there. So I continued to lie there and took a nap until Big Mama's round came along. This was not her real name, just what most inmates called her. No one bothered to write me the tickets because they knew this is what I wanted. Not her. She wrote the tickets, and I finally had enough to leave, even though I did not know what to feel or think. I did not want to go to level four, and I did not believe I was really going. It was about seven o'clock when I was given all the tickets that I had caught that day. There were seven tickets, all for being out of place and disobeying direct orders. The sergeant informed me that I would be leaving soon. Shortly after, on her way home, Ms. Jacks walked up to me. She sat down right next to me so close I felt very uncomfortable. She said that she had found Roy's letters and that she knew the truth. I did keep a few of his letters. I looked at her and said, "Oh, Ms. Jacks." She just shook her head at me. When she got up to walk away, I asked her where I was going. She said to level four. I put my head down; she got up and walked away.

To be continued.

ABOUT THE AUTHOR

Mr. Ready enjoys spending time with friends and family, While Motivating and inspiring those around him. He is a proud father of three, working towards the release and publication of the breaking shackle series. While incarcerated he received a certificate in electronics trade from St. Louis Michigan in 2009. In 2013 he received a certificate in basic manufacturing trades from Muskegon community college. He has attended grand rapids community college along with Ashford University studying communications. Also attending Baker community college studying Business in his free time he enjoys meditation, yoga, reading and playing chess.